KV-635-988

Critical Guides to French Texts

105 Montesquieu: Lettres persanes

Critical Guides to French Texts

EDITED BY ROGER LITTLE, WOLFGANG VAN EMDEN, DAVID WILLIAMS

MONTESQUIEU

Lettres persanes

Christopher Betts

Senior Lecturer
University of Warwick

Grant & Cutler Ltd
1994

© Grant & Cutler Ltd 1994

ISBN 0 7293 0376 4

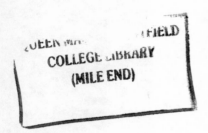

QUEEN MARY FIELD
COLLEGE LIBRARY
(MILE END)

I.S.B.N. 84-401-2138-5

DEPÓSITO LEGAL: V. 523 - 1995

Printed in Spain by
Artes Gráficas Soler, S.A., Valencia
for
GRANT & CUTLER LTD
55–57 GREAT MARLBOROUGH STREET, LONDON W1V 2AY

Contents

Prefatory Note

The references that I make to the text are to individual letters, not in any specific edition, but following the numbering (Letter I to Letter CLXI) used in the two critical editions by Adam and Vernière, which are listed as *1* and *2* in the bibliography, and to which I refer when discussing whole or fragmentary letters left unpublished by Montesquieu. Students using older editions may find some slight differences in the numbering of the letters, especially towards the end of the work. Of the cheaper editions currently available, those in the Folio, Garnier-Flammarion and Livre de Poche Classique series can be recommended. References in the form (*26*, pp.63–64) are to the numbered items in the bibliography at the end of this volume.

1. Preliminaries

The *Lettres persanes* in 1721 was a work published anonymously in two small volumes in Holland, and brought for sale to Paris. What the book's many buyers saw on the title-page is that it was published in Cologne by Pierre Marteau. They would also have noticed that, like other French books published outside France (and some inside), the volumes lacked a *privilège*, the official licence to publish. A *privilège* usually certified that a book had been approved by the censors as containing nothing detrimental to religious belief, loyalty towards the throne, or public decency; its absence implied that the *Lettres persanes* did not respect these values. The false imprint — it concealed the name of the publishing house of Desbordes in Amsterdam — conveyed the same message. Pierre Marteau was a pseudonym adopted by publishers to signify that a book's content would not be welcome to the authorities. Thus the appearance of the *Lettres persanes* gave an impression totally different from that of a modern edition, as did virtually all the other leading texts of what we now call the French Enlightenment. Books by Montesquieu, Voltaire, Rousseau and Diderot come to us consecrated by the reputations of their authors, and bedecked with introductions, notes, and other scholarly apparatus. All that readers in 1721 had to go on was the text, the suspect title-page, and the patently unreliable information given by the 'translator'.

It was not uncommon for books to be anonymous; authorship was only gradually becoming a reputable activity, having suffered in the seventeenth century from aristocratic prejudices against working for money. Even so, the anonymity was another indication that the book might not please the orthodox. Governmental control of publication included serious penalties for offenders (though booksellers and printers suffered more often than writers), and even during the Regency of Philippe d'Orléans (1715–23), when the régime was milder than before or after, it was not in Montesquieu's best interests to be known as the author of audacious opinions. He may have been needlessly cautious: in the event, no action was taken against his book. However, there is evidence (*25*, pp.85–88) that his later candidature for the Académie française was hindered, when Cardinal Fleury was in power, because the Cardinal did not care for some passages in the *Lettres persanes*. He had been informed of them, according to Montesquieu's notebooks, by a Jesuit, Père Tournemine. They were probably the remarks about the Pope in Letter XXIV, but the Académie itself was also treated unflatteringly, in Letter LXXIII.

The provocative combination of disguise and advertisement in the words on the title-page is prolonged through the text. From the introduction, which came first in the 1721 editions (the 'Quelques réflexions' placed before it in modern editions date from 1754), we learn that the writer is 'un homme grave', but he immediately claims not to be the author, merely a translator. This is almost an admission that the Persians are fictional. Nonetheless, they are foreign, which frequently makes the scope of their observations difficult to assess. When they profess to be shocked by European customs, should we interpret it as an attempt to be realistic about foreigners in France, or as a method of dissimulating criticism? When they praise the customs of their own country, are they being patriotic, or making veiled recommendations to their French readers? We have to make up our own minds, the ambiguities being inherent in the indirect mode of expression chosen by Montesquieu.

The 'Quelques réflexions sur les *Lettres persanes*' do not keep up the Persian pretence, but they too need to be carefully interpreted. The 1754 edition in which they first appeared came out soon after the book had been the target of a full-scale attack by one Abbé Gaultier, otherwise unknown to history, on the grounds that the letters were anti-religious. His book, *Les 'Lettres persanes' convaincues d'impiété*, of 1751, was an offshoot of the much larger controversy surrounding Montesquieu's *Esprit des lois*, published in 1784. This great masterpiece of political, social and legal thought aroused much opposition from the pious, the *parti dévot*. With the benefit of hindsight, Gaultier was able to perceive the seeds of later impiety in the earlier, less serious work. Montesquieu, by now aging and in poor health, was disinclined to court controversy, and wrote defensively. The *Réflexions* explain at rather too great length that the 'traits que bien des gens ont trouvés trop hardis' were not intended to offend, but merely to reflect the Persians' surprise. This is not convincing. Consider a notorious passage in Letter XXIV. Rica has the idea that the Pope is a magician, who can make the King, Louis XIV, believe anything: 'il lui fait croire que trois ne sont qu'un, que le pain qu'on mange n'est pas du pain, ou que le vin qu'on boit n'est pas du vin; et mille autres choses de cette espèce'. Being a Muslim, Rica is supposed not to realise, in his innocence, that the three and one are the persons of the Holy Trinity, and the bread and wine the 'species' of Holy Communion; nor that he has — unintentionally, of course — made a pun by using the word *espèce*; nor that the dogmas in question are the most fundamental in Catholic doctrine, rather than the material for exercises in magic.

If we believe the *Réflexions*, we should regard Rica's misunderstanding as the result of foreign ignorance. But in 1721 the Frenchman supposedly responsible for translating and publishing the letters must have known perfectly well how shocking Letter XXIV was (and can still be): had he not wished to make fun of the Pope, the King and the dogmas, he would have omitted the passage, but chose to include it. In any case, the anonymity, the concealed Dutch publisher and the absence of a *privilège* show that at the time of publication Montesquieu himself fully realised the need for precautions.

However, it is difficult to gauge how great the degree of audacity was. Before publishing his book, Montesquieu showed it to his former teacher, a broad-minded Jesuit, Desmolets. He, apparently unperturbed by the features that Gaultier was to find 'trop hardis' thirty years afterwards, forecast correctly that 'cela se vendra comme du pain'. We must assume that one factor in its success was that during the Regency many readers enjoyed mockery at the expense of the late Louis XIV and his relationship with the Pope.

The work sold so well (again, according to the *Réflexions*) that the publishers in Holland went around asking everyone they met to write more Persian letters. It may have been Desbordes, not Montesquieu, who followed up the book's success and put out a second edition within the year, again using the name Pierre Marteau, but with a curious rubric on the title-page: 'Seconde édition. Revue, corrigée, diminuée et augmentée par l'Auteur'. It lacks thirteen letters, mostly concerning Usbek's seraglio, that are in the first edition, but includes three that are not. It might perhaps have been intended (as was argued by Barckhausen, the work's first modern editor) for the large French-speaking Protestant market, strait-laced about sexual morality and unlikely to have appreciated the seraglio story. Changes in Letter XXIV support this, since the jibes against the Pope and the Catholic doctrine of Holy Communion were retained, but the words concerning the Trinity were deleted. Edgar Mass (*20*, Ch.II, especially pp.135–38) argues persuasively that the so-called 'second' edition, with its 140 letters, was in fact meant by Montesquieu to be the first: the first edition as published had 150.

The mysteries of the curious 'enlarged and abridged' edition may never be fully resolved, but its altered text is further evidence of the delicacy of religious and sexual topics at the time. No manuscript of the *Lettres* has survived that might cast light on these matters, except for Letter LXXVII, which was added for the 1754 edition (and some manuscript pieces unpublished by Montesquieu, which modern editors place in appendices). We shall not often have to confront textual questions, but I should mention that many of the later variants, found in the 1754 edition, tone down the vivacity of the original text. Letter LXXVII is a case in point. It is Ibben's response, not present in 1721, to Letter LXXVI, which argues in favour of suicide — against the Church's prohibition. Ibben, however, seems (though none too clearly) to be justifying laws against suicide. The 1754 letter is therefore more in line with Catholic opinion than Usbek had been.

Faced with the *Réflexions*, then, which admit that some passages may offend but explain them away as being merely the ideas of 'Persians', I think that it is natural to be sceptical. We should regard the Persian dress of the letter-writers essentially as a literary device, or 'mask' to use Starobinski's term (*26*, pp.63–64), enabling more or less audacious criticisms to be made with impunity. The *ancien régime* being hostile to freedom of publication, authors devised a variety of stylistic techniques, usually involving some kind of foreign disguise, in order to express their views while not openly flouting the censorship regulations.

Montesquieu does not merely give the letter-writers Persian names; he includes a whole Persian background — not strictly necessary if disguise was his only aim — complete with an extended story about Usbek's seraglio, two other short stories, and 'un nombre innombrable' (a favourite phrase, probably intended to seem extravagant and Oriental) of passages about Persian and other Eastern customs. Many readers of 1721 would have been familiar with the work on which the Orientalism of the *Lettres persanes* was certainly modelled. It too was an anonymous letter-series, commonly known as 'L'Espion turc' or 'L'Espion dans les cours'. Its Genoese author, Gian-Paolo Marana, had begun to publish it in 1682. Appearing in both English and French, it was not completed until 1699, and was often reprinted, under varying titles. Like Montesquieu's work, it was mainly devoted to reports about France, but they came from Mahmut, the Turkish spy, whose business it supposedly was to keep the Ottoman Emperor informed about the doings of the Christians.

Marana's Orientalism was comparatively superficial; from him Montesquieu took the habit of transposing European terms into Asiatic, mainly in the domain of religion. Monks become 'dervis', hermits 'santons', and so on. The Muslim lunar calendar is Westernised by giving the twelve months Muslim names, and ignoring the differences in the count of days: January becomes Zilcadé, February Zilhagé, March Maharram, April Saphar, May and June Rebiab I and II (a misspelling for Rebiah), July and August Gemmadi I and II, September Rhegeb, October Chahban, November Rhamazan, and December Chalval. For 1711 and 1712 Montesquieu hesitated whether to begin the year in the Persian way with Maharram, then decided against it. At this level he was not impeccably accurate; there are one or two errors. For instance, in several letters he writes *mollak* instead of the more exact transcription *mollah*, and in Letter CXLI *beiram*, meaning public prayer, appears regularly for *harem*. But as regards research into the political, social and religious background he is in a different class from Marana, and from any of the other writers who borrowed the Oriental guise. Although his knowledge is second-hand — very few West Europeans penetrated beyond Turkey; as the *Lettres* make clear, travel between West and East took months — but by Vernière's count (*2*, xix–xxviii) information from at least eleven books can be certainly found in the letters concerning the Orient, and if we include the sources for the letters about Europe and those that are no more than probable, the total goes up to well over fifty. In Letter LXXII Montesquieu indulges in some self-mockery, satirising the know-all who has read books by Chardin and Tavernier, but his own study of Chardin, the best of his informants, must have been thorough. He learned enough to make historical as well as verbal transpositions; Letter LXXXV discusses religious persecution during the reign of Louis XIV by way of parallel events in Persian history.

The purpose of the Oriental guise cannot only have been to provide local colour or to amaze the reader with horrifying or titillating scenes from Persian life. The letters also perform a task more befitting 'un homme grave', namely as complete a comparison as possible between Eastern and Western societies. The investigation continues throughout the book, and is probably the reason for the lengthy section about matters Persian that begins it. By the time that Usbek and Rica arrive in Paris we already know a good deal about the country they have left behind, and further knowledge is fed into the later letters, giving substance to the many judgements made about the relative strengths and weaknesses of the two civilisations.

In presenting so various a work, selectivity is essential. The opinions expressed by the Persians (not always in agreement) are on politics, religion, society, morals, sexuality, economics, history and literature, a list that is not exhaustive. Montesquieu's intellectual ambitions were all-embracing, as is evident from the huge scope of the *Esprit des lois*, and in the earlier work he also displayed brilliant literary gifts in satire and narrative. The variety, which has impressed every commentator on the *Lettres persanes*, was certainly deliberate. Although the letters are often in brief groups of two or three, unified by a narrative incident or topic of discussion, it is the contrasts as we pass from one letter to the next that will strike the reader; in this perspective the letters' opening sentences are rewarding to study. However, the opening does not always indicate the main topic, since even within the space of a single short letter Montesquieu seems to take pleasure in straying from one subject to another. Letter LXXXII begins with a joke about monks, but is mainly on conversational bores; Letter CXXVII, with the sudden death of a great king, but is on the bad influence of ministers.

In order to find a way through this labyrinth, I shall take up a suggestion made in the *Réflexions*, that — even apart from the story of Usbek's seraglio — the letters form 'une espèce de roman'. In the course of their stay, the Oriental travellers' attitudes change, which forms the outline of a story, though of an unusual kind. The key to the change is the division established by Vernière (2, p.xix) at the end of the reign of Louis XIV, marked by Letter XCII. Before this comes the expository section of the seraglio story; the journey to France; and the Persians' first bewildered impressions. Their surprise merges into satirical observation as they grow accustomed to French behaviour. The division at Letter XCII is symbolic rather than exact, but the monarch's death does seem to mark a major turning-point, as I shall argue in the chapter on history. The letters dated afterwards, during the Regency, are more reflective than satirical, and the tone is more serious than before, becoming pessimistic in the last letters about France and stormy in the Persian dénouement.

The approach I adopt is designed to avoid implying that there is one central idea in the *Lettres persanes* to which all else is related. The much-studied remark in the *Réflexions* about 'une chaîne secrète' has encouraged speculation that some hidden plan can be discovered which will make everything fall into place. In my view the remark means only that the letter-form and the narrative outline of his work allowed Montesquieu to include all kinds of material without bothering too much whether it was exactly coherent. However, a certain utilitarian attitude is often present, if utility can be defined very widely as whatever conduces to the public good, and in the chapters on the satirical and reflective letters I argue that this somewhat diffuse attitude is prevalent in the work, though it cannot be said to dominate it.

2. From Persia to France

The subjects of the early letters are two: Usbek's motives for leaving his country, and the seraglio he leaves behind, his wives and eunuchs. His motives are explained in the autobiographical Letter VIII, which reveals that he is, in French terms, a high-ranking nobleman, driven away by court intrigues, having made enemies by his integrity and plain speaking. He also wishes to study, 'm'instruire dans les sciences de l'occident', the motive that is both his and Rica's in Letter I. Their story will partly be that of their Western education. Rhédi too, the nephew of Usbek's close friend Ibben, wishes to be educated, and goes to Venice (Letter XXV). The letters he exchanges with the others illustrate what they learn; in Letters CV and CVI, for instance, the lesson concerns the value for civilisation of technological advance. From the beginning it seems that European knowledge is superior. As the travellers pass through Turkey, they note the desolation of the country (Letter XIX), except in Smyrna, or Izmir, which 'les Européens' have made rich and powerful. It is in Smyrna that they meet Ibben.

The seraglio is a less straightforward matter, as is shown in a modern study by Alain Grosrichard (15). Montesquieu's treatment includes the outline of a narrative, but is also a mixture of psychology and sociology, portraying imaginatively the situation about which Montesquieu had read in Chardin: a number of women, wives and slaves, are kept in confinement by castrated men. Many of the letters are of the kind recommended in Montesquieu's *Réflexions*, in which the writer 'rend compte soi-même de sa situation actuelle'. Thus, from Zachi's Letter III, we have some insight into the feelings of a woman competing in a highly-charged beauty contest for the favour of Usbek's attentions, and from Letter IX into those of a man physically unsexed but still tormented by lust. In his eyes, Usbek is 'un homme heureux', but the word must apply only in the physical domain, since Letter VI discloses Usbek's anxiety, jealousy and suspicion. He is almost as much a victim of the seraglio system as the wives or eunuchs. Rica is unmarried and carefree.

In their sociological aspect, the letters about the seraglio convey that its purpose is to ensure what Usbek calls the women's 'vertu': chastity and fidelity, again in an exclusively physical sense. It also ensures that the husband's sexual needs are invariably met. In Letter VII, Fatmé explains very clearly how frustration works to the benefit of the male. Besides being imprisoned and sexually deprived, the women are indoctrinated from youth, as we learn from Letter LXII. Even so, the husband's sexual monopoly is threatened. The wives may resort to lesbianism, unmistakably hinted at in Letters IV and XX; Letter XX also reproves Zachi for some kind of sexual activity with one of the eunuchs. Their intended role is of course exclusively disciplinary. Usbek puts it very strongly in Letter XXI, his second response to the misdeeds that provoke these revelations of his tyranny: 'qui êtes-vous', he asks rhetorically of the eunuchs, 'que de vils instruments que je puis briser à ma fantaisie [...] qui n'êtes dans le monde, que pour vivre sous mes lois, ou pour mourir dès que je l'ordonne?'

The fictional side of the *Lettres persanes* has not always been taken seriously by critics, some of whom have entirely ignored it, or mentioned it with regret, as if (like its successor *Le Temple de Gnide*, a short lyrical evocation of love, published in 1725) it was unworthy of the author of the *Esprit des lois*. In more recent criticism (e.g. *10, 15*) it has been given much fuller attention, often because of its quasi-political overtones, although it is generally admitted to have defects. The inquisitive interest in female sexuality can seem merely salacious, for instance in Letters III or VII, and later when a Circassian slave is bought, in Letter LXXIX. The main complaint, however, concerns characterisation. The wives and eunuchs are so little differentiated that Montesquieu himself seems to lose track of their identity; Adam lists some of the inconsistencies (*1*, p.xix). The criticism he makes is justified to some extent, although it would be anachronistic to expect miniature Emma

Bovarys or Anna Kareninas in Usbek's unfaithful wives. The reason is partly that the wives' individuality is indeed much reduced by the conditions of their existence. The term sex-objects applies exactly. They are distinguished only inasmuch as each illustrates one of the few possible responses to their situation: continued frustration, it seems, for Fatmé (who is lost sight of later); lesbianism for Zéphis; exhibitionism or perhaps sexual play with a eunuch for Zachi. Zélis's distinguishing feature is that she has a daughter. The course taken by Roxane, whose ferocious chastity Usbek praises in Letter XXVI, is not revealed until the end; until then, she appears to be obedient and virtuous, because Usbek's appreciation of her is all we have to go on. For the time being it is she alone whose conduct seems to vindicate the seraglio system.

Usbek's character also is determined by the requirements of the small society which he owns. If it is to function efficiently he, like the eunuchs who exercise authority in his name, must be constantly suspicious. He is bound, too, to suffer jealousy, which for him is not the turmoil of knowing that his wife loves another man, but the fear that his rights of possession may be infringed. When they are, or seem to be, punishments are extreme: the white eunuch Nadir is executed (Letter XX). Worse will follow, Letter XLVII reporting that two complete strangers have been killed for approaching too near to the wives during an expedition to the country. The necessity for control may also be the only reason why Usbek writes of his love in the letters to his wives. The first letter to Nessir (which in the so-called 'Seconde édition' was the first letter of all) says that he does not love them. From his remarks to Zachi and Roxane, in Letters XX and XXVI, his 'love' seems to be a kind of reward for virtue.

Alarmed by the incident between Zachi and Nadir, Usbek's last act in protection of his seraglio is to send back Jaron (Letter XIX). Thenceforward the series of letters about France will be punctuated at intervals by reports of various happenings in Persia — the plot to castrate Pharan, the dangerous visit to the country, the dreadful behaviour of Suphis (Letters XL–XLII, XLVII, LXX) — which reinforce the impression of insecurity and violence. A

complete contrast is made, while the Persians are still travelling to
Europe, by two short series of letters. In the first, beginning the
important letters about the Troglodytes, Mirza asks Usbek about
happiness. He has vainly sought advice from mullahs, 'qui me
désespèrent avec leurs passages de l'Alcoran' (Letter X); what he
means is shown in the second series. Here, when Usbek in turn asks
advice in turn from a mullah, querying the Muslim prohibition on
eating pig-meat, he is treated to a disgusting tale, ascribed to the
Prophet, which gives the mythical origin of the ban (Letters
XVI–XVIII).

Apart from bringing Islamic tradition into disrepute, with
implications about similar prohibitions in the Old Testament, the
three letters show that Usbek already has sufficient independence of
mind to question received ideas. In his own answer to Mirza
(Letters XI–XIV), he displays optimistic and liberal beliefs that are
much at variance with his attitudes within the seraglio; what he says
in respect of marriage among the Troglodytes, for instance, could
scarcely be more unlike what we have read from him as a Persian
husband. The interpretation of this divergence is doubtful. We can
simply say that Montesquieu did not succeed in unifying the
emotional and intellectual sides of his main character; or if we
prefer the view that the human personality need not be unified and
coherent, we can say that Usbek is one person as a husband, his role
being largely dictated by the fixed institution of the seraglio, and
another when he is able to develop his ideas freely.

The fable of the Troglodytes teaches the value of social
cooperation. Even in its sentimental moments, it makes a welcome
relief from the bitterness and strife of the seraglio. First we have to
be shown, not without humour, that unbridled selfishness leads to
national disaster. The surviving parents inculcate the main social
and economic message: 'l'intérêt des particuliers se trouve toujours
dans l'intérêt commun' (Letter XII). It follows that if individuals
work for the common good they will also serve their own interests,
as is demonstrated by the second generation of Troglodytes. The
nation and all its members thrive prodigiously. By the end we
realise that Mirza's question in Letter X, whether happiness comes

from pleasure or virtue, is a false dilemma: pleasure and virtue are not mutually exclusive, since the Troglodytes achieve both.

Usbek's 'morceau d'histoire' has attracted much commentary, largely because it perfectly expresses a typical eighteenth-century ideal, enlightened self-interest. In Usbek's formulation, this is not only the cynical idea that we often benefit by being (apparently) unselfish, but the bias of a radical reform of society. However, it remains an ideal, not a policy. When, in Letter XIV, the fable comes closer to reality with the election of a ruler (and even more so in a further letter about the introduction of money, left in manuscript — see the appendices of modern editions), the ideal and the narrative seem to waver, as if Montesquieu cannot see how to adapt Troglodyte virtue to the practicalities of life in society.

In its historical context, the allegorical message about cooperative endeavour is also a repudiation of an attitude typical of the seventeenth century, pessimism about the selfish and violent tendencies of human nature. Speaking very generally, the attitude can be found both in the Jansenist emphasis on Original Sin (Pascal's 'le moi est haïssable' derives from this) and in the political thought of Thomas Hobbes, whom Montesquieu is often considered to have had in mind when composing the letters on the Troglodytes (6). Basic issues are at stake, then, the letters raising questions with which anyone reflecting on the individual and society should be concerned. Within the context of the *Lettres persanes*, the function of the allegory is to instil the assumption that man is a social animal. It is a principle treated humorously in Letter LXXXVII, but underlies Montesquieu's whole outlook. Individuals are invariably seen as members of their society, not (for instance) in the way that the religious seventeenth century had seen them, as beings whose main concern was their Christian salvation, nor as complex psychological subjects, the conception made familiar by nineteenth-century novels. Indeed, 'individuals' is almost too strong a term; the Troglodytes are even less differentiated than Usbek's wives, and in the letters about France particular men and women are defined by their social positions and roles.

For the Persian travellers, the frontier between Islamic East

and Christian West comes between Smyrna, the home of Ibben, and
Italy, where the port of Livorno provides them with their first
surprise: the 'grande liberté' of Italian women (Letter XXIII).
Amazingly, they are permitted to look out from their houses at men
passing by. (The comparison to make is with Fatmé's remarks in
Letter VII.) Otherwise, Livorno is only a staging-post on the way to
Paris, which Usbek calls 'le siège de l'empire d'Europe'. The
ignorance, bewilderment, and occasional naïvety of the Persians are
a feature of this part of the work. The resulting literary effects are
often imitated from Montesquieu's predecessors, especially Marana,
but are more entertaining and ingenious. Letter XXXII, for
example, forces the reader to share Rica's lack of understanding
until the end. When Rica goes to see a show, in Letter XXVIII, he
thinks that what he has come to watch is the progress of the love-
affairs being played out in the boxes, a normal meeting-place for
lovers, while it is in the *foyer* that 'comédie' is seen — exaggerated
French politeness. The plays themselves, it seems, are only temporary interruptions to the actresses' own love-affairs.

As for the Opéra, the goings-on there are revealed in the first
letter-within-a-letter, from one of the chorus-girls or dancers, whose
reputation as *femmes faciles* was well-established. But here the
humour of surprise has serious undertones, Letter XXVIII making
an extreme contrast, as regards sexual *mores* in France and Persia,
with Usbek's Letter XXVI, to Roxane. Momentarily at least, it
might seem that Usbek's strict views on chastity have some
justification. The opera-girl's plight is not really comic, since her
pregnancy will put her out of work; she is reduced to looking for a
rich protector, which according to Jean Meyer (*21*, p.282) was often
an economic necessity for women working in theatre and opera.

It seems to be deliberate that all the early letters about France
are from Rica, who has not written before. Usbek takes longer to
acclimatise himself. Rica's opening description is the intricate and
celebrated Letter XXIV, the most notorious passage of which I have
mentioned in Chapter I. It begins innocently enough on the tribula-
tions of a pedestrian, Rica playing the standard comic role of the
victim. This is a false start, the letter soon becoming less innocent

as we read of Louis XIV's power over his people and that of the Pope over him. The second half of the letter is all about Jansenism, though Rica seems not to be aware that it was the target of the Pope's 'grand écrit' (the bull *Unigenitus* or 'Constitution'), nor that the 'ennemis invisibles' surrounding Louis everywhere are the Jansenists. By the end, the king is much less formidable than at first; the sense that his power is unreal prevails throughout. Not only is it based on dubious financial expedients — the sale of public offices, manipulation of currency values — but he also fails to impose his will on the women of the kingdom, and cannot find the invisible enemies. (That Rica the Muslim should approve of the Constitution because it prevents women from reading the Bible — the practice was that only the *paterfamilias* should do so — does not mean, of course, that we too should approve; rather the contrary.)

One problem nowadays with Lettre XXIV, apart from the topical allusions and the pseudo-naïve disrespect for Christian beliefs, is that it inextricably combines religious and political considerations. The modern Western convention (but not the Islamic one) is that religion and politics should be separate, and this is probably the view that Montesquieu wishes to suggest, since the opposite situation underlies much of the letter and produces bad results. The King is the political chief of the nation, but allows himself — so it appears — to be dominated by the Pope; when Louis tries to enforce the Pope's declared wishes, he fails. At the time, everyone realise that Jansenism, which we now tend to regard as a purely religious movement, had an important political dimension, or rather that religious non-conformity could and often did overlap with political non-conformity. This was something that Louis did all he could to stamp out. He succeeded to a large extent, but Jansenism revived during the eighteenth century. In the social circles in which Montesquieu moved, the administrative nobility or *noblesse de robe*, support for Jansenism was widespread, and to my mind there is no doubt that, through Rica, he is indulging in feelings of satisfaction that the movement has defied the combined efforts of King and Pope. But Lettre XXIV's humour also suggests, simply because it is humour, that the whole business of putting down religious opinion by authoritarian measures is laughable. We shall encounter the same humorous indifference to religious matters in many other letters.

Separate treatment is given to the Pope and King subsequently, in Letters XXIX and XXXVII, but they follow the line laid down in Lettre XXIV. The beginning of Lettre XXIX is just as disrespectful as before about the Pope, 'une vieille idole', and for the same reason: his undue power, now past, over secular monarchs. It was possible to employ such language in Catholic France about the supreme head of the Church because of the strength of the tradition known as Gallicanism, the belief that the Church in France should manage its own affairs independently of the Vatican. The principal theme of the letter is religious contradiction and conflict, summed up in a particularly sharp comment which depends on the idea that Christendom is a 'kingdom': 'Aussi puis-je t'assurer qu'il n'y a jamais eu de royaume où il y ait eu tant de guerres civiles que dans celui du Christ'. Rica backs this up with a satirical attack on the Inquisition in Spain and Portugal, the first of many such attacks on intolerance in Enlightenment literature; the target is the same in the rather less mordant Lettre LXXVIII. Modern readers may need to be told that Rica's feelings of satisfaction that Islam is a tolerant religion, one that 'n'a point besoin de ces moyens violents pour se maintenir', with Montesquieu's own note in support, is derived from Chardin's testimony about the East.

Usbek's Lettre XXXVII, the sequel to the political side of Lettre XXIV, lists 'contradictions' in Louis XIV's behaviour which carry the same critical charge as the earlier letter's list of astonishing things. Louis is irrational in his choice of mistress and minister (that he had secretly married Madame de Maintenon was still not public knowledge), and in religion, public relations, economics, and the allocation of rewards to his officers. Here his policies turn to the lunatic: 'aussi lui a-t-on vu donner une petite pension à un homme qui avait fui deux lieues, et un beau gouvernement à un autre qui en avait fui quatre'. What Usbek is describing is rule by caprice, the universal habit of dictators, which he castigates more frankly when writing about the rulers of Persia in

Lettre CII. In Lettre XXXVII, the accusation of dictatorship is made in one of those masterly understatements, a feature of Montesquieu's satirical style, which have more venom than is immediately apparent: 'on dit qu'il possède à un très haut degré le talent de se faire obéir'. Rica seems to approve of Louis, because Louis approves of the Ottoman Emperor and 'notre auguste sultan'; but in other letters (Lettres XIX and XXXIII, for instance) we are told that these monarchs are dangerous tyrants.

The Persians' first attitude to France is one of alienation, less deeply felt by Rica than Usbek. When they have settled in, and are able to make detailed comparisons with Persia, the contrast between East and West is for a while the dominant element in their letters, until it gives way to a strain of satire which does not depend on the contrast. During this time — about a year, going by the letters' dates — the news from Persia implicitly reinforces the sense of difference, since it always concerns events of a kind that could not happen in Europe, and illustrates what to Europeans is a callous disregard for suffering.

After some months, Usbek reconciles himself in some respects to French customs. On arrival, he had written to Nessir in Lettre XXVII about his despondent state, just after his expressions of horror about French women in Lettre XXVI. But on religion he is more open-minded. Comparing Islam and Christendom in Lettre XXXV, he is pleased to find many resemblances, and casts doubt on a rigorous Muslim belief — another example of intolerance, of the kind he presumes that his cousin the monk might favour — that Christians are fit only to be damned; he hopes, in a flight of lyricism, that the differences will be transcended and all religions united. Lettre CXXIII is to repeat the wish. Meanwhile Rhédi has just arrived in Venice and is being a little intolerant himself, but is delighted with the opportunities for education (Lettre XXXI); in response (Lettre XXXIII), Usbek writes a very balanced comparison between the two cultures on the subject of alcohol and opiates.

Usbek is still learning with indignation about French society in Lettre XLVIII, eighteen months after reaching Paris; he meets a would-be Don Juan who provokes him to thoughts of violence ('Si vous étiez en Perse [...] vous deviendriez plus propre à garder nos dames qu'à leur plaire'). Rica, on the other hand, has already come to terms with the consequences of the freedom enjoyed by French women. In Lettre XXXIV (from Rica in the 1721 editions; Montesquieu later weakened the distinction between the two Persians by ascribing it to Usbek) he compares them with Persian women, much more appreciatively than Usbek in Lettre XXVI, and goes on to criticise the psychological effects of harem life generally. The national contrast governs Lettre XXXVIII also. Rica understands that Persian husbands may be concerned about their wives' fidelity, but notes that the French are not. The issue is whether men should exert their superior strength, 'l'empire que la nature leur a donné sur les femmes', in order to control women's conduct. The Asian assumption that they should do so is countered by French arguments from which Rica distances himself slightly, as a Muslim should ('le Prophète a décidé la question'), but which he presents favourably; to enforce obedience is 'une véritable tyrannie'. Usbek would not write thus, but Rica has no seraglio.

A question emerges from all the contrasts: do men from one country differ fundamentally, or only superficially, from those who live in another? The issue is raised directly by Rica's conclusion in Lettre XXIV: 'les hommes du pays où je vis, et ceux du pays où tu es, sont des hommes bien différents', and dramatised in the delightful and much-quoted ending of Lettre XXX. Rica decides to put on Western costume, and thus passes unnoticed unless his nationality is mentioned, whereupon he in his turn causes surprise: '"Ah! ah! Monsieur est Persan? C'est une chose bien extraordinaire! Comment peut-on être Persan?"' European parochialism is brilliantly expressed in the question, its language setting the unsolvable problem of the relation between the general and the particular. Linguistically, 'on' cannot be Persian, or any particular nationality, because the word means man in general, the abstract, non-specific person beloved of seventeenth-century writers, about whom universal truths of human nature can be stated, as in La Rochefoucauld's *Maximes*. Yet the fact remains that Rica and Usbek are Persians, and much of what they say depends on it. The issue, put in a pedestrian manner, is whether our nature varies, because it is determined by our social environment, or is the same in all human beings, whatever their circumstances. Lettre XXX sums up the contrasts and comparisons typical of the early letters by raising this problem, and in the sequel we are given some materials from which to construct an answer.

3. Satire

The formlessness of the *Lettres persanes* defies the literary historian to classify the work; no one genre seems to fit. However, the Latin word *satura* meant a miscellany or medley, something like our satirical revue, treating a variety of subjects, often topical, with derisive humour. It is tempting therefore to think of the *Lettres persanes* as satire, especially since Diderot gave the same name to his *Neveu de Rameau*, another unclassifiable work, except that the *Lettres persanes* is long and contains much serious reflection. Satires in modern literature, especially when in verse, have usually been short, consistent in tone, and limited in subject-matter. However, borrowing the idea of satire rather than the word itself, we might apply the modern term miscellany, thus indicating at least the variety of content and style. The same label could be attached to several works by Voltaire, such as the *Dictionnaire philosophique*. As for satire proper, it plays a major part in the *Lettres persanes*, as in some of Molière's plays or Voltaire's *contes*, but does not dominate. It merits a chapter of its own, especially since the more obviously satirical letters are bunched together.

The section of the miscellany that is primarily satirical, then — for satire is also found before and after — begins once the Persians have settled in, and fades out as the Regency supersedes the reign of Louis XIV; or in terms of numbers, runs approximately from Letter XLV, on the alchemist, to Letter LXXXVIII, on noblemen. Most of the letters in question come from Rica. Usbek is capable of satire, but is not often flippant, and when he mocks it is with greater weight. His Letter XLVIII may be regarded as a transition from the period of the Persians' first reactions to that of satirical observation of French society. In it he still needs to be instructed about the people he sees, and is treated by a French acquaintance to a series of short literary portraits, a genre highly developed in a work which Montesquieu is certainly imitating here, La Bruyère's *Caractères* (2, e.g. pp.100, 111, 114). But finally Usbek meets and is much angered by the *homme à bonnes fortunes*, and light social satire becomes fierce denunciation.

Readers often find satire difficult. It can be a matter of temperament, for some will dislike the satirist's aggression and destructiveness. Personal circumstances can play their part; the old find it harder than the young to laugh at Molière's harsh parents, and women may object more than men to some of the *Lettres persanes*. Political attitudes, in the widest sense, are also relevant. As James Sutherland writes, satire 'has always been unwelcome to people in authority' (*English Satire* (Cambridge, 1962), p.133); it is necessarily subversive of respect for established values and institutions. We have already seen in Lettres XXIV and XXIX how religious authorities can be belittled. Technically too, satire can present problems, because it works essentially by implication. In order to appreciate the satirist's attack, you have to 'see what he's getting at', as with jokes. This is perhaps why satire often works best in a small and closed society, where allusions and prejudices are shared.

I shall begin with the last and least contentious of the potential obstacles, and distinguish between satire's particular weapon, implication, and the blunter instrument of direct denunciation, as found at the end of Letter XLVIII. As this letter shows, the two can coexist in the same piece. At its lowest, denunciation is no more than insult and invective, and is always nearer to being simple opinion than a type of literary expression. Letter L begins with opposite kinds of opinion, panegyric (the modest and virtuous persons whom Rica admires) and denunciation (those with little ability and much conceit). The continuation is pure satire — a little conversation-piece or *tableau* in which the bore is allowed to tell us in his own words how excellent he is in all respects. The implied criticism here is almost self-evident; in order to grasp it, all we have to do is to note the contradiction in 'je ne me loue jamais; j'ai du bien, de la naissance, je fais de la dépense, mes amis me disent que j'ai quelque mérite; mais je ne parle jamais de tout cela'. That we as

readers make the connection, however, without having it spelt out
for us, is an essential part of the technique.

Another essential is that we should be persuaded to enjoy the
discomfiture of the person satirised. In Letter L the task is virtually
done in advance, since most people object to conceited bores, but in
other cases the satirist may have to take greater care. The remarks
already discussed about Louis XIV in Letters XXIV and XXXVII
are camouflaged as surprise and misunderstanding, since to attack a
king, even if he was dead, ran counter to the *ancien régime*'s deep-
seated feelings of loyalty to the monarchy. The clergy was another
matter. Anticlericalism had a long history before the *Lettres
persanes*, and could be indulged in even by those of genuine
religious sensibilities. A number of letters (Letters XLVI and
LXXXIII, for instance) show that the Persians take religion
seriously, but there is much mockery of clerics. One of the portraits
in Letter XLVIII is of a fashionable director of conscience, con-
sulted by society ladies about their amatory problems; in the next
letter a Capuchin monk meets with a sharp rebuff when he seeks
funds for missionary work in Persia, which Rica considers pointless;
a casuist, in Letter LVII, explains to a no less indignant Usbek how
to palliate sinful conduct.

Anticlerical satire is found also in some later letters: in Letter
CI, a sequel to the passage in Letter XXIV about Jansenism, Usbek
annihilates an ignorant bishop who supports the other side, the
Jesuits; and in Letter CXXXIII Rica asks for assistance in a monastery library and meets another ignoramus ('Bien des gens me font
de pareilles questions; mais vous voyez bien que je n'irai pas lire
tous ces livres pour les satisfaire'). Like the fool in Letter L, these
characters are full of self-satisfaction, which contributes to our
pleasure when they are discomfited. Sometimes, as with the
directeur or the monastery superior in Letter CXXXIII, they are
condemned by more subtle techniques of mockery. One is false
praise from the satirist. Usbek's friend in Letter XLVIII is most
appreciative of the *directeur*'s value: 'il fait la douceur de la vie
retirée; petits conseils, soins officieux, visites marquées; il dissipe
un mal de tête mieux qu'homme du monde; il est excellent'. In

Letter CXXXIII, the ignorant monk condemns himself by his actions: on hearing the dinner bell, he disappears 'comme s'il eût volé'.

Defining the exact sense of the satire can be difficult, because implied meaning is often non-specific. A comparatively sympathetic letter, Letter LXI, about 'un ecclésiastique' whom Usbek meets in Notre-Dame, helps to focus the implied accusations in the anticlerical satire. He himself is not satirised, for he admits the deficiencies of the clergy. They are ineffective in preserving the moral standards of society ('corriger' the *gens du monde*) and seem doomed to doctrinal intolerance, suffering from 'une certaine envie d'attirer les autres dans nos opinions'. This is a definition of proselytism, the activity of the missionary monk who annoys Rica in Letter XLIX. The *ecclésiastique* in Letter LXI has at bottom the same attitude as Rica, that it is useless to try to make converts: 'Cela est aussi ridicule que si on voyait les Européens travailler, en faveur de la nature humaine, à blanchir le visage des Africains'.

The charge against the missionary, that of uselessness, applies in various ways to other clerical personages. The praise given to the smiling *directeur* in Letter XLVIII means that the services he provides have no real value, and the monk whom Rica meets in the library serves no purpose at all, even though he is the head of his society. With the bishop in Letter CI, the position is not much different: authoritarian but incompetent, he shows himself unworthy of his important position. Both he and the monastery superior have socially useful roles to perform, but they fail to do so. At bottom this is what the cleric of Notre-Dame says in Letter LXI, when he deplores the clergy's failure in moral education. Members of the priesthood could be valuable members of society; the satire directed against them (usually those of higher rank) invariably draws attention to ways in which they fall short of the ideal. The worst of them is the casuist, who accordingly brings down on himself the fiercest rebuke, his purpose in life apparently being to condone immorality.

Several of Montesquieu's satirical techniques — the self-revelations by the victims, the miniature dramatic scenes or

tableaux, the observer's reactions of criticism or false admiration —
are connected with the basic literary device of the *Lettres persanes*,
that of *persona* or the mask (see *27*, p.63). The words mean the
same, *persona* (often preferred in American criticism) being originally the tragic or comic mask put on by Roman actors. The device
has always been a favourite with satirists, permitting them to
present as natural and plausible a point of view that might be
excessively hostile for an author speaking in his own person. Swift's
Gulliver and Voltaire's Amabed (and even the German Candide in
certain respects), Goldsmith's Chinese, and many others, enabled
their creators to discard the habits of thought with which they had
grown up, and observe their society as if they were new to it.

v. imp

Montesquieu's use of *persona* changes. In the early months of
the Persians' stay, when contrasts and comparisons with their own
country are frequent, their Persian-ness is very noticeable, but
becomes much less so later, except that as foreign visitors they are
entitled to make enquiries, about those whom they meet, which
would seem implausible coming from a native Frenchman.
Gradually, the masking technique develops; expressions of naïve
surprise or indignation in the *persona* of a foreigner evolve into a
coherent attitude to French society for which *persona* seems irrele-
vant. In the religious satire that I have just been discussing, we can
see this process under way as Rica's and Usbek's concern for moral
and social values becomes clear. There is nothing inherently Persian
about Usbek's hostility to the tricks of the casuist's trade, even
though he ends with an obviously 'Persian' remark. In the group of
letters we now come to, those devoted to the social life of Paris, we
find Rica — it is usually he — developing an attitude for which
utilitarianism seems the most suitable name. In this context utility is
not the narrow practical value of fitness for a specific purpose, but
relates to the individual's worth as a member of society.

Letter LXXXVII is a good example. The obsessive maker of
visits (whose energy Rica exaggerates and pretends to admire — the
mock epitaph at the end is a marvellous example of the satirist's
false praise) regards the activities of himself and his like as
essential. Rica does not, as he implies ironically: 'Ils sont toujours

empressés, parce qu'ils ont l'affaire importante de demander à tous ceux qu'ils voient, où ils vont, et d'où ils viennent'. Plainly, they ought to be doing something more useful. To go back to one of the early letters, the same view is expressed in Letter XXXVI by Usbek, more openly, about the *beaux esprits* whom he had heard debating the greater or less excellence of Homer: 'ce qui me choque [...] c'est qu'ils ne se rendent pas utiles à leur patrie, et qu'ils amusent leurs talents à des choses puériles' (*amuser* here is broadly the equivalent of 'waste').

The same theme is present in several letters (Letters XLVIII, L, LIX, LXXII, and LXXXII) that evoke gatherings in the *salons*, the reception rooms in town and country residences belonging to those wealthy and hospitable enough to provide friends and acquaintances with regular opportunities for meetings and conversation. In the *cercle* or *compagnie* or *société* that the Persians describe, social success could be won or lost; many a career was made by the talents required in order to shine in the *salons*. Letter LIV is extremely revealing about what was involved, the would-be *bel esprit* overheard by Rica being overcome with the fear of failure, since public attention counts above all else: 'il y a plus de trois jours que je n'ai rien dit qui m'ait fait honneur; et je me suis trouvé confondu pêle-mêle dans toutes les conversations, sans qu'on ait fait la moindre attention à moi, et qu'on m'ait deux fois adressé la parole'. Fortunately for him, he has a friend to advise him: 'Fais ce que je te dirai, et je te promets, avant six mois, une place à l'Académie', and they concoct an elaborate plan. The implied criticism again relates, I think, to the use of talent: it is that entry to the Académie should not depend on the trivial successes of *salon* conversation. Personal merit is also an issue in Letter LXXXII, according to which success goes to those who possess such things as blond wigs and snuff-boxes. 'Un homme de bon sens', says Rica, perhaps with a touch of pique, 'ne brille guère devant eux'.

He has also had to give best to the famous 'décisionnaire' (Rica's own word) of Letter LXXII, a perfect satirical sketch of yet another conceited man. His fault is not so much that he is vain, but that he is anti-social; his encyclopaedic knowledge stifles conversation. The letter illustrates a general characteristic of satire: that it appeals to the reader as a member of a particular social group. At its widest, the group may be the public at large, but is often more restricted. In Letter LXXII, as in Letters L and LIX, the appeal is to everyone who has met for the purposes of conversation and had the purpose defeated by an egotist like the *décisionnaire*. Elsewhere, we are invited to share in the mockery of mediocre writers or Parisian saleswomen on the basis that, like Rica, we have hoped to benefit from a book but in vain (Letter LXVI) or have visited a tourist trap (Letter LVIII). Often we can appreciate the satire only if we are prepared to enter the role that is prescribed for us, and which may be more unusual today than in 1721. In two passages in Letter XLVIII we are expected to look down on poets and rich *parvenus* from poor backgrounds; but here the satire may not be effective, because the rationalist and aristocratic prejudices to which Montesquieu appeals have largely disappeared, and with them the complicity between author and reader on which satire necessarily relies.

When, as is normal in the *Lettres persanes*, the author treats his readers simply as members of the public, social utility is the value to which he appeals. Rica's Capuchin, in Letter XLIX, is sent packing because his project is 'très utile' to the world, ironically speaking, like the arguments about Homer in Letter XXXVI. In Letter XLV, Rica's anger is due partly, no doubt, to having been rushed out of bed too early, but also to the uselessness of his visitor's alchemical investigations. Here as in many other letters the target is also stupidity — the Persians can certainly be said to be intellectual snobs — but social utility is so frequently evoked that I am inclined to see it as the main principle underlying the satire. Through the spectacle of activities without uses, we are led to value those that serve society at large, or those of the 'bon citoyen', in a phrase from Letter XLVI. This is why the judge is attacked in Letter LXVIII. He is ignorant and untroubled by it, which would not matter if his social duty did not call for expertise. He is therefore a bad citizen, useless in the broad sense, a legal version of the clerics in Letters CI and CXXXIII. It is in such ways as this that satire,

Law

which can seem empty or negative, conveys a positive message which is all the more effective for being concealed.

When women are the object of Rica's satire, his view that ←— people should not waste their time is much modified by gender. Often he writes simply as a man, and for male readers, making perennial masculine complaints about extraordinary fashions and feminine vanity, but displaying great virtuosity in the rejuvenation of such well-worn themes. Letter LII constructs a narrative of such artificial precision as to appear to be almost the demonstration of a law relating to women whose ages differ by twenty years. In Letter LI a curious myth about Russian women, that they like to be beaten, is the basis for a topsy-turvy account of Russian marriage, according to which violence proves love. The degree of fantasy is hardly less in two letters of a later date, Letters XCIX and CX, on the caprices of fashion and the lives of society women: a woman pictured in the dress of a previous generation looks as strange as a Red Indian squaw; the feminine obsession with social appearances compels women to enjoy the most boring of parties, unlike Rica, who goes to sleep.

In these passages the satire is close to comedy, and to me — speaking as a man — seems not to amount to a serious attack. Hostility to women is much greater in Boileau's Satire X, or its model in Juvenal. But in many other passages in the *Lettres persanes* the implied accusation, also traditional, is that women are unchaste, and in these cases one at least of the male voices seems to be in great earnest. As we have seen already, Usbek does not regard conjugal fidelity as a laughing matter. When he writes about women gambling, in Letter LVI, their purpose is first to 'favoriser une passion plus chère' and then to 'ruiner leurs maris'. Finally even love is seen as a threat, because of the power it gives to women. This letter is more denunciation than satire. By contrast, in the letter immediately preceding, Rica is able to joke at length about jealous husbands. It is the wives who are at fault originally, it seems, but Rica's genial tone considerably reduces the gravity of the accusation.

Rica values sexual constancy much less than Usbek, and

women's freedom more. In Letter LXIII he says that their social equality is a clear advantage for men, bringing openness rather than division. However, he then complicates the issue, describing the spread of the habit of *badinage* from its natural home, the boudoir, into important public affairs: 'on badine au Conseil, on badine à la tête d'une armée, on badine avec un ambassadeur'. In another context (Letter XCVIII, on financial matters), Usbek is inclined to think well of a minister who makes jokes, but the ending of Letter LXIII seems not to imply approval. The impression is much strengthened by Letter CVII, when it is not merely modes of speech that are affected by the influence of women, or *féminisation*, the term used by Jeanne Geffriaud-Rosso (*13*, pp.347f.; her view, though well argued, seems to me to overstate the case against Montesquieu). In this letter, the passage on women begins by being facetious about the rivalry between royal mistresses and royal confessors, but most of it is an elaboration of a standard eighteenth-century joke: that a young man can best achieve advancement in his career by becoming the lover of an influential woman. 'J'entendis un jour une femme qui disait: "Il faut que l'on fasse quelque chose pour ce jeune colonel: sa valeur m'est connue; j'en parlerai au ministre"': the pun on *valeur*, sexual prowess and military valour, tells us that if the young man is promoted it will be for the wrong reason (rather like the *bel esprit* in Letter LIV). If we care about the public good or, to be specific, the good of the army, we should not view this prospect with favour. Here we are being addressed, not as males sharing a joke at women's expense, but once more as members of the public, who should be concerned at the deleterious effects of women's power.

Rica ends his letter by alluding to complaints that in Persia a few women are all-powerful (which is somewhat puzzling, in view of the relentless subordination of Usbek's wives), and adds: 'C'est bien pis en France, où les femmes en général gouvernent.' The criticism might be grave if Usbek made it, but Rica's tone is light; I think that we are expected to read his remark as comic overstatement. Occasionally the shift from gender-based humour to concern over the public welfare is found in other letters about women, such as Letter XCIX, on fashion. Most of it consists in the humour of exaggeration, but at one point Rica notes that architects have been obliged to alter doorways so as to accommodate women's wide skirts (the famous hooped *paniers* of the time). 'Les règles de leur art ont été asservies à ces caprices', he says, his disapproval here seeming quite strong. Despite moments like this, the satire of women is to my mind less weighty than that directed at the clergy; it is nearer to the satire of the types met in *salons*, who are ridiculed not because they threaten the welfare of society as a whole, but because they are a nuisance within the limits of the social grouping in which they appear.

Moreover the satire of women is tempered by the many passages in which they appear in a favourable light; the legendary charm of Parisian women certainly works its magic on Rica, if not on Usbek. In Letter LVIII, even when Rica is writing of the less reputable feminine trades in Paris, it is hard to tell whether he is admiring or reproving. The relative hostility of the satire on women and that directed against the clergy can be gauged from the masterly Letter CXXV, a mixture of argument and fiction with satirical overtones, in which the horror intrinsic to the subject of the story, the Hindu custom of suttee, is dissipated by comedy. The widow who intends to follow tradition and immolate herself on her husband's funeral pyre is portrayed as foolish, but the villains of the piece are the Brahmin priests (whom Montesquieu by an oversight calls 'bonzes', the term for their Buddhist counterparts). It is they who have indoctrinated her with the idea of self-sacrifice; when she changes her mind, her motives are hardly admirable, but it is her put-down of the priest that provides the real satisfaction of the tale. Rather than feminine caprice, the satirical target seems to be the danger of religious bigotry.

Montesquieu treats some subjects mainly through satire, some mainly in the reflective arguments with which Chapter 5 is concerned, and some by both means. As regards women, the *Lettres persanes* contains few discussions (except in Letter XXXVIII), and there are virtually none about the institutions of French social life, although the *salons*, cafés, and other places of assembly are the settings for numerous letters. The topic of religion, however, is almost equally balanced between satirical and reflective letters, and this mixed method is also well exemplified in the letters about nobility, which will be my last topic in this chapter.

The subject was a delicate one for Montesquieu, who held a high position in a society which was ordered by family and rank rather than wealth. He belonged to the *noblesse de robe*, ennobled for service to the King in the administration of justice; it had somewhat less prestige (except in its own eyes) than the *noblesse d'épée*, which owed its privileges to service on the battlefield. There were many other divisions within the nobility, but they could unite in disdain of the pursuit of mere money, trade being regarded as an occupation unfit for a nobleman. Even so, some official posts which made their possessors noble could be bought. The *Lettres persanes* uneasily recognises the importance of money, which was growing steadily as France began to move from an agrarian to an industrial economy, but regards it, and its pursuit, as disreputable. In this respect the last paragraph of Letter XCVIII is typical, both of the work and its time, although its disparaging attitude was to be modified during the course of the eighteenth century.

Usbek's rank, transposed into French terms, is even higher than his creator's. He is from 'the sword' and is entitled to appear at court: a *grand seigneur*, able to look down on the petty arrogance of the aristocrat in Letter LXXIV, who has nothing in his favour except his poor opinion of everyone else. (He somewhat resembles the racist colonials of Letter LXXVIII, whose pride is based on being — more or less — white-skinned.) Usbek's closing remarks in Letter LXXIV are a pointer to what true nobility consists in: military and diplomatic leadership. But in Paris, in Letter LXXXVIII, he finds that equality rules; 'la naissance, la vertu, le mérite même de la guerre' (another brief overview of the traditional noble qualities), do not confer prestige. Here Usbek's remarks on equality are an ironic attack on the decline in status that the nobility suffered after Louis XIV had made it dependent on court patronage. The elderly aristocrat in Letter LIX, living on a government allowance, illustrates the process, which is also described, more

bitingly, in Letter CXXIV. When Usbek mentions with approval
that in Persia nobility is earned only by 'ceux à qui le monarque
donne quelque part au gouvernement', the implied suggestion is for
'aristocratic reform' under the Regency, in Haydn Mason's phrase
(*19*, pp.59–73); the nobles felt that their rightful share in administrative power had been denied them by Louis's reliance on ministers
taken from the lower orders of society. Letter CXXXVIII mentions
with praise (probably undeserved) the *conseils* on which the Regent
gave the nobility full representation.

The satirical Letter LXXXVIII, preceding two reflective
letters, combines with them to form an essay on the ethos of the
noblesse d'épée. (The next, Letter XCI, added only in 1754, scorn-
fully attacks the Persian envoy who in 1715 had miserably failed in
the nobleman's duty — as described in Letter LXXIV — of
representing his monarch and his country.) Letter LXXXIX is on
gloire, the exalted ideal of fame striven for by the aristocratic heroes
of Corneille's plays; Letter XC on duelling, which was the most
notorious expression of the nobleman's code of honour. The tone is
a little equivocal. As a *grand seigneur*, Usbek ought to approve of
glory and duels, but he has reservations. The desire for glory is
'cette noble passion', but also an 'heureuse fantaisie' — fortunate
because it serves a purpose useful to the state, that of inspiring
soldiers with courage. Glory is not, therefore, an end in itself, as it
had been in Corneille. On duelling, Usbek is more openly critical,
considering it legalistically as a method of settling differences,
almost as if it were an alternative to going to law. His attitude is
much more that of the robe, that is to say of Montesquieu, than of
the sword which he is supposed to represent.

The same is true of the dialogue in Letter LXVIII, when Rica
reproves the *homme de robe* who cannot be bothered to study his
legal authorities. Rica does not here speak as the *noble d'épée* who
scorns the pen-pushing lawyer, for the legal function itself is taken
seriously; his criticism is rather, as I have mentioned already, that
the judge is unworthy to perform it. With this reproach we return to
the criterion of social usefulness that prevails in the satirical letters.
Gloire is seen in a utilitarian way in Letter LXXXIX, since it is

useful militarily, and a related letter, Letter LXXXIV, ends with the wish that the names of soldiers who die in battle should be preserved in 'des registres qui fussent comme la source de la gloire et de la noblesse'. Such comments imply patriotism, but also confirm that service to the nation is coming to seem more important than inherited social position.

Such satire as there is in the passages concerning nobility is mild, which in my view is characteristic of most of the satire in the *Lettres persanes*. The Persians are more constantly critical than La Bruyère, a relatively conformist writer, but despite the anger that they sometimes feel, their remarks are usually moderate, and lack the destructive power of Voltaire's attacks. There is little or none of the 'savage indignation', *saeva indignatio*, of the fiercest satirists in other literatures, Juvenal and Swift. Montesquieu learned from Pascal's *Lettres provinciales*, as can be seen from his Letter LVII, but his predecessor's deep feeling is usually absent; the ending of the letter briefly arouses it. The harshest passages in the *Lettres persanes* take the form not of satire, but of denunciation, and are most often found in the reflective letters which predominate in the second half of the work, such as Letter CXVII on monasticism or Letter CXLVI on financial affairs. One reason for the impression of mildness may be the equivocal tone that I have mentioned in connection with Letter LVIII: the Persians often appear to take satisfaction from the exercise of their satirical wit, and to forget criticism in the pleasure of the description. The portraits of the *décisionnaire* in Letter LXXII, or the bishop in Letter CI, seem to be meant to arouse enjoyment rather than disapproval.

4. History: the View from 1721

The relationship between a literary work and its historical background is seldom conveniently simple, and the *Lettres persanes* is no exception. Although it is firmly embedded in its time, we cannot make a list of historical events and find them tidily reflected in the letters. Usbek and Rica are not chroniclers or reporters, unlike their predecessor, Marana's Turkish Spy, who often notes contemporary developments. Moreover, there is no exact correlation between the subjects in Regency history that modern historians find important and the subjects on which the Persians choose to comment. For instance, the atmosphere of the period, after the heavy intolerance and severity of the latter part of Louis XIV's reign, was one of permissiveness, the behaviour of the Regent and many of his subjects being quite uninhibited by the conventions of Church or morality. It may look at first as if the mood is shared by Montesquieu. The eroticism of the seraglio stories is unmistakable, and Rica reports entertainingly on the prevalence of extra-marital affairs in Letter LV. However, there is a great contrast between, for instance, the drunken orgies indulged in by the Regent's entourage (*12*, pp.131f.) and the discreet portrayal of Persian sexuality in the *Lettres*. Or to take another case, the letters testify to the increasing freedom and importance of the social life of Paris, but they do not mention one of the main causes: that the Regent had abandoned court life at Versailles, with the result that 'la ville', Paris, became the single social centre of France. Again, an important innovation in foreign policy under the Regent was to create strong links with England (the enemy under Louis XIV), at the expense of the traditional alliance with Spain. In Montesquieu we shall not find the least reference to the realignment; there is perhaps just a hint that things have changed in Letter LXXVIII, a splendid piece of satire aimed at Spain, and Letter CIV, which discusses English political ideas with respect.

Hence if we are to claim, as is often done, that the *Lettres persanes* contain the best literary portrayal of the few remarkable years, from 1715 to 1723, during which Philippe d'Orléans held power, we shall have to formulate our claim with some care. The novelty and freshness that is almost palpable at the time is strong also in Montesquieu's writing, but we shall not find much history in the ordinary sense. Just two important happenings are fully treated, in very different ways. The main one is the change of reign itself, in 1715, when the king-to-be, Louis XV, was still a child; the other is the sensational progress of John Law's 'Système' a few years later, the first occasion in French history when a purely financial operation caused upheavals throughout society.

The change of reign is built into the *Lettres persanes* in a number of ways, so pervasively that the difference between the present régime and the past comes to seem a constant preoccupation. Even today the break in 1715 seems radical: histories of the century tend to start in that year, the epoch-making death of Louis XIV coming soon after the treaties of Utrecht and Rastatt, in 1713 and 1714, which ended decades of war throughout Europe, and settled the balance of power until Napoleon (or even, in a larger perspective, until 1914). In the *Lettres persanes* we find something more meaningful than dates, though less definite: an awareness that a major political change has occurred, and a new era begun. For readers in 1721, the effect of reading the letters dated up to 1715 must have been that they concerned a vanished time. The impression given of the previous reign is that it belongs firmly to the past; no longer relevant, but only a memory.

The reason for this is partly that the length of Louis XIV's reign is often emphasised and associated with age. 'Le roi de France est vieux', says Usbek in Letter XXXVII; 'nous n'avons point d'exemple, dans nos histoires, d'un monarque qui ait si longtemps régné'. He adds that Louis has an eighty-year-old mistress and an eighteen-year-old minister. In the context, the reference to youth does not rejuvenate the aged monarch, but makes him seem senile. Antiquity is a feature of the preceding letter also, Usbek recalling that on his arrival in Paris a trivial controversy was going on about 'un vieux poète grec, dont, depuis deux mille ans, on ignore la patrie, aussi bien que le temps de sa mort'. Letter XLVIII's gallery of portraits includes one of an old soldier, who lives in the past, 'il respire dans les temps qui se sont écoulés'; the various nostalgic types in Letter LIX, among them 'des vieilles femmes', 'un homme qui paraissait accablé de goutte', and 'un vieux seigneur', hark back to the great days of Louis XIV and are mocked at for doing so. The satire in Letter LII is aimed at the old women, not the young. The contrast is made sharper in Letter CVII, dated 1717 and devoted to 'le jeune monarque'; it repeatedly connects youth with the future Louis XV and age with the preceding reign.

There is no awed respect for the past, then, but rather irreverence — the irreverence of the young for the old. Another important theme in the portrayal of the preceding reign is that of war. The implication is that, since 1715, the time for making war is over: this is how Montesquieu registers the fact of the peace-treaties. Militarism is an intrinsic element in Letter XLVIII's portrait of the old soldier and a number of other passages. Rica admires the Invalides in Letter LXXXIV (for once paying tribute to Louis XIV), but he also brings 'toutes ces victimes de la patrie' to our attention. The veterans of Louis's wars are now 'guerriers débiles', soldiers whose fame is forgotten. Letter LXXXIX, one of the group on aristocratic matters, suggests that the motivation of troops by the hope of glory in monarchies (such as France) is less effective than motivation by patriotism in republics (such as Holland, another enemy before 1715, though ostensibly Usbek is writing about ancient Greece). The military power of the Tartars is evoked in the second letter on Russia, Letter LXXXI, dated 1715; the moral seems to be that conquest alone — in which the Tartars far surpassed Louis — is an empty achievement.

In letters dated after 1715, passages about war are fewer, and it becomes literally a peripheral subject: battles take place at the edges of Europe in Letters CXXIII, CXXVII and CXXX. The Austro-Spanish war of 1716–17 is merely a matter for humour in Letter CXXX, which also contains letters from a comically absurd author. He plans two books, one proving 'que Louis le Grand était le plus grand de tous les princes qui ont mérité le nom de *Grand*', the other that the French have never been defeated in battle. In other words, another of the differences between past and present established by Montesquieu is that a militaristic ethos of glory and sacrifice has now been superseded, the new mood being one of ironic scepticism about war and its purpose.

We find a similar contrast between past and present in the religious sphere. Again Letter XXIV is important: it establishes the assumption that conflict and persecution had been the norm under Louis XIV, when the Persians had arrived. In 1713, Usbek opens Letter XLVI with the observation: 'je vois ici des gens qui disputent, sans fin, sur la religion', and in Letter LXXV, dated early in 1715, 'La religion est moins un sujet de sanctification, qu'un sujet de disputes'. Letter LXXXV, a little before the letter recording Louis's death, is one of the few that refers to an event of the preceding century, the King's most notorious and far-reaching act of religious intolerance, the Revocation of the Edict of Nantes in 1685. Aimed at the sizeable Protestant population, the Huguenots, it imposed the obligation on all French citizens to be Catholics, and the result was enforced conversions and large-scale emigration. Montesquieu camouflages these events as incidents from Persian history, first a proposed measure against the Armenians, 'd'obliger tous les Arméniens de Perse de quitter le royaume, ou de se faire Mahométans', then the persecution and flight from Persia of another religious minority, the Gabars. The culmination of Letter LXXXV is an attack on intolerance, 'cet esprit de prosélytisme [...] cet esprit de vertige, dont les progrès ne peuvent être regardés que comme l'éclipse entière de la raison humaine'.

An ironically different judgement on intolerant policies is given by the fatuous cleric of Letter LIX, looking back thirty or forty years: 'vous parlez là du temps le plus miraculeux de notre invincible monarque. Y a-t-il rien de si grand que ce qu'il faisait alors pour détruire l'hérésie?' Letter LX, mainly about the Jews, also recalls 1685 and religious dissension, but in another quite different manner; the style is elaborately casual. This is probably because the criticism applies explicitly to France, instead of being disguised, as in Letter LXXXV: 'on s'est mal trouvé [...] en France d'avoir fatigué des Chrétiens dont la croyance différait un peu de celle du Prince'. The Jews also used to be persecuted, says Usbek, but things have changed: 'Ils n'ont jamais eu dans l'Europe un calme pareil à celui dont ils jouissent', a situation of which we are certainly meant to approve, since the letter ends with another plea for tolerance. Although Letter LX is dated 1714, the contrast it makes between past strife and present peace applies exactly to the reign of Louis XIV and the Regency. In the letters after 1715, almost nothing can be found about religious intolerance. This is one matter, then, in which the *Lettres persanes* clearly reflects, or speaks for, its time, tolerance being the policy pursued by the Regent.

In sum, the implication is that the reign recently over had been a mixture of senility, the empty glories of war, and religious persecution. To this unflattering picture Letter CXXIV, a sequel to Letter XXXVII, adds a pointed critique of Louis XIV's court. The letter's own history is significant: it was omitted from the first edition, presumably because Montesquieu regarded it as too bold; it appeared in the second 1721 edition with the date of January 1715, which is appropriate to its content; but in the cautious 1754 edition, and in modern ones, it has the date of 1718, which veils the reference to Louis. It mainly consists of an imaginary royal decree: the insatiable demands of the courtiers are to be financed by ordering the rest of the King's subjects to cut expenditure on their families. The court is portrayed as a place of wanton idleness, made famous by military success and the intrigues of women, 'quelques-unes même très surannées'.

Whether Montesquieu's portrayal of Louis XIV's reign is accurate is not in question here, because what we find in the *Lettres persanes* is not so much history as a partial and satirical image of the past. In that sense, it is a genuine record of the previous reign as perceived in 1721. When we move to what Montesquieu's readers must have viewed as the present, the few years before 1721, the focus changes. Things become relevant in a manner not to be found earlier, not merely because they are recent, but because they may be important in the future — the future of Montesquieu himself, and his readers, known to us but not to them.

This explains why more attention is given to topical events in the later letters. It is natural for the past to diminish in significance as it recedes; in the *Lettres persanes*, events further away from the time of writing are treated more vaguely. For the years 1712 to 1715 there is an almost complete lack of contemporary detail. This does not fit well with the fiction that the letters were written at the same time as their dates, but is entirely comprehensible when we realise that they were not. (Letter XCI, dated 1715, appears now to be reporting on a contemporary event, the arrival of the Persian envoy, but is not found in the 1721 editions; Montesquieu added it in 1754.) The only current event that the Persians bother to mention during these years, in Letter XXIV, is another example of intolerance, a decree issued against Jansenism, the papal bull 'Unigenitus', known as the Constitution. Montesquieu gets the date wrong, making it earlier than it was, 1710 instead of 1713, and treats it with flippancy. Even the death of Louis XIV, which in retrospect seems so significant, is only briefly treated in Letter XCII, in rather conventional rhetoric. Not until the end of 1718 do current events come to the fore.

The reasons for their inclusion are various. One series of allusions concerns the transmission of power on the accession of a new ruler — a moment of high risk in a monarchy. The old king was dead, but how long would the new king live? For contemporaries it was a source of anxiety, the young Louis XV being in poor health. Letter CVII reflects on the dangers to France and Europe were the young Louis XV to die, and Letter CXXVI reports (in the disguise of news from Mogul India) the outcome of an unsuccessful Spanish plot to oust the Regent if Louis did not survive. Two letters about Sweden (Letters CXXVII, CXXXIX) are also inspired by changes of reign, though here the subject seems to be a pretext to moralise.

In other topical letters, Montesquieu is preoccupied by the growing social importance of money, which he sees with disapproval and associates with a decline in the influence of his own class, the *noblesse de robe*. His concern is especially prominent in the letters about Law's 'Système', as in earlier ones about finance and financiers. The tone is sober and serious, like that of the letters expressing disquiet about Louis XV. Despite the sense of satisfaction that the reign of Louis XIV is at last over, the joy and relief that are often said to typify the Regency are hard to discern here, Rica's high spirits being overshadowed by Usbek's caution. On the *noblesse de robe*, Letter XCII reports that the Regent's first actions as ruler brought the *parlements* some renewal of authority, but the tone is elegiac, as if this promising development could not last; and in Letter CXXXVIII another remark about the compromise form of government in 1715–18, the 'conseils', on which the aristocracy had more power than under the old king, begins with high praise and ends in pessimism: 'ce ministère est peut-être celui de tous qui a gouverné la France avec plus de sens: la durée en fut courte, aussi bien que celle du bien qu'il produisit'.

The vague impression of foreboding about the future becomes much stronger in the letters about the 'Système'. Their main themes are instability, as in a fragment left in manuscript which describes the Regency generally (*1*, p.409; *2*, p.339), and the emptiness of wealth when it is gained solely from financial operations. Throughout the *Lettres persanes*, financiers — who under the *ancien régime* were often 'tax farmers', private individuals to whom the right of levying the nation's taxes was 'farmed out' by the government — are seen as social pests. In Letter XLVIII one of them is vulgar and boastful, while Letter XCVIII gives expression to the well-bred jibe against them, that they are merely jumped-up lackeys. Such is Usbek's contempt that for once he descends almost to coarseness. He is referring to the frequent marriages between impoverished aristocrats and the daughters of rich financiers; 'leurs filles', he says, 'sont comme une espèce de fumier qui engraisse les terres montagneuses et arides'. Another source of the outrage aroused by the 'Système' is that it has allowed servants to enrich themselves and buy their way into the nobility; the satirical ending of Letter CXXXVIII puts the idea in exaggerated form.

In outline, Law had two interrelated enterprises, a bank and a trading company. France had no national bank at the time (nor for many years after), and Law's *Banque générale*, founded only in 1716, succeeded so well that in 1718 it was made into the *Banque royale*. For a while, it even seemed capable of bringing some order into the chaos left in the finances of the kingdom by Louis XIV. The other part of the 'Système' was the creation in 1717 of a huge company, trading in goods from the colonies then ruled by France in northern America. Later its operations became worldwide. The 'Compagnie du Mississippi', as it is known, was financed by the bank, but was intended in turn to produce profits which would support the credit that the bank advanced. Money flowed in from the sale of shares in both enterprises; the share-price shot up, and there were scenes of frenzied speculation, the most sensational side-effect of the 'Système'. Rica alludes to them in Letter CXXXVIII when he writes of 'ceux qui viennent de quitter leur livrée dans une certaine rue', the newly-rich servants.

At the height of his power Law was given control of the nation's finances, his projects including plans for paying off the national debt and reforming the extraordinary methods by which taxes were raised. His operations, however, became more and more complicated (partly because rival financiers made big claims on his bank for cash payments), and led eventually to massive alterations in the values of shares and notes — a dramatic new version of financial chaos. Together with the inflation of share prices, these desperate manoeuvres are the subject of Montesquieu's satire in the exactly detailed fable which is presented as a 'Fragment d'un ancien mythologiste' in Letter CXLII. The letter is perhaps the oddest example of the disguises of contemporary history in the *Lettres persanes*. The heart of it is an early metaphor for what we call inflation: Law's shares become the air in balloons, and the bank's credit belongs to the 'Empire de l'Imagination'. Law himself becomes the son of the wind-god Aeolus. The 'fils d'Eole' finds that the nation does not have a sufficiently strong imagination; in other words, confidence in the share prices waned. As it did so and his bank became unable to meet its commitments, Law tried various expedients, notably in an edict by which the value of the shares was to be reduced by almost half ('souffrez que je vous ôte la moitié de vos biens', in the fable). This, in May 1720, was the last straw; disturbances broke out in Paris and the edict was revoked ('Je m'aperçus hier que mon discours vous déplut extrêmement. Eh bien, prenez que je ne vous aie rien dit'). Shortly afterwards, dismissed from his post and almost penniless, Law had to flee the country.

Montesquieu makes no effort to judge Law's projects as equitably as modern historians, who trace various long-term advantages deriving from the 'Système' (*5*, pp.297–99). For him, writing soon after the crash, the effects are uniformly bad. He takes the side of the Paris Parlement, temporarily banished to Pontoise in 1720 for its refusal to accept one of Law's measures; in oratorical style, Letter CXL depicts the *parlementaires* as martyrs to the truth, persecuted for their efforts to inform the Regent of the wretched state of the country ('apporter au pied du trône les gémissements et les larmes dont ils sont dépositaires'). Their fate recalls that of Usbek years earlier (Letter VIII). In Letter CXLVI he denounces the bad example set by 'un ministre sans probité', Law, to 'une nation naturellement généreuse', France disguised as India (perhaps because the definitive name of Law's company was the Compagnie des Indes). The denunciation is fierce and unrelenting; it seems justified when we read of the wave of crime and immorality produced, in the opinion of contemporaries, by the lust for money that the 'Système' encouraged (*2*, p.323; *17*, pp.39–41). The accusations made by Usbek centre on the damage done to family fortunes when debts are settled in devalued money; family capital at the time was often advanced to individuals who paid it back over a long period at low interest (*21*, pp.199–200). The scenes in Letter CXLVI are of the capital being destroyed by being paid back in a lump sum, but in the devalued notes of Law's bank. It was legal (the notary, 'un homme noir', is there to supervise), but Montesquieu plainly thinks it immoral.

The letter ends with a phrase about the 'affreux néant' into which the present generation has cast itself. Letter CXLVI is the last about France. Looking back from the twentieth century, the picture of the Regency that it completes can seem somewhat puzzling, for it is at odds with the period's usual modern image: an optimistic and exciting prelude to many decades of economic expansion and peace. The view that the Persians transmitted in 1721 was not at all optimistic. The main impression is one of insecurity. It derives partly from the theme of instability and change found in Letter CXXXVIII and elsewhere, and partly from the choice of topical subjects found in the letters. I have mentioned the concern caused by the health of Louis XV as a child; in 1720 he was seriously ill, as Montesquieu's readers would have been well aware. Besides the upheavals caused by the 'Système', the other source of public alarm shortly before the publication of the *Lettres persanes* was the plague in Marseilles and Provence. It may have been chance that made Montesquieu begin the series of letters on depopulation with some remarks on the catastrophic plagues of history (Letter CXIII), though if so the coincidence is remarkable, but in 1721 his comments would have seemed ominous. The last remarks of this series of letters are also pessimistic: 'chez les peuples misérables, l'Espèce perd et quelquefois dégénère. La France peut fournir un grand exemple de tout ceci' (Letter CXXII). Since Usbek's own future is grim (Letter CLV), the cheerful atmosphere of the earlier letters has entirely disappeared, to be replaced by dismay and doubt. We may if we wish see this as a lesson that even the most penetrating of observers can be wrong, given the almost constant improvement in the standard of living in France during the rest of the eighteenth century, but if we are to take the *Lettres persanes* seriously as a record of the time we must, I think, conclude that the view in 1721 was unsettling. For the Persians at least, and presumably for others also, the outlook in France gave cause for anxiety rather than confidence.

5. Discussions: Justice and Utility

Reflections and discussions on general questions are as typical of the later letters about France as satire is of the earlier, taking the report of the King's death in Letter XCII as a symbolic dividing line between the early and the late letters. The division is only approximate, several reflective letters being found before this point, including the three most important letters discussing religion, and, as I have mentioned, four letters (Letter LXXIV and Letters LXXXVIII to XC) treat the subject of nobility partly through satire and partly by direct discussion. The questions directly tackled in the later letters sometimes produce miniature essays, as in the pair of letters, Letters XCIV and XCV, on international law, with special reference to war, while the letters on depopulation (Letters CXI to CXXII) are generally regarded as being originally a dissertation, split up by Montesquieu into portions suitable for inclusion in a letter-series. However, since all the discussions, whether confined to a single letter or spread over several, are now parts of a larger whole, the interpretative issue that confronts us is whether the conclusions they reach on the specific questions add up to a coherent general philosophy. The problem is one to which no two commentators on the work are likely to give the same answer. Waddicor's (*32*, pp.38f.) is that the leading principles are relativism and rationalism, combined in justice and morality. The argument I will pursue is that Montesquieu's reflections are based on two concepts, those of justice and utility, which are normative in nature and overlap to some extent, since in the political domain utility corresponds to the public good.

Of the two, the concept of justice is the simpler to approach, because it is the object of a number of explicit statements and a celebrated definition. Almost the first of Usbek's opinions to be recorded, by Mirza in Letter X, is that justice is for men 'une qualité qui leur est aussi propre que l'existence'. Letter LXXX contains an analogous statement: 'le prince', says Usbek, using the standard term for a head of state, 'est la loi même'. In Letter LXXXIII, it is the nature of God that is defined: 'S'il y a un Dieu [...] il faut nécessairement qu'il soit juste'. Although the formulations differ, their convergence is remarkable; the two closely related ideas, those of justice and law, are said to be essential in God, kings, and men.

Montesquieu elaborates his idea by way of conceptual oppositions between justice and its contraries. The justice of men, or *équité*, as it is also called, is explained in the Troglodyte letters as the contrary of self-interest. The first generation of Troglodytes all but perishes because of their extreme selfishness (Letter XI); their successors flourish because they follow justice (Letter XII). Justice seems here to be the equivalent of economic cooperation. The pattern is the same in the letter on God. Men can act unjustly out of self-interest, but God, having no needs and no self-interest, must follow the precepts of justice: 'dès qu'on suppose qu'il voit la Justice, il faut nécessairement qu'il la suive'. However, some theologians take another view, it seems, and portray God as 'un être qui fait un exercice tyrannique de sa puissance'. The subject here must be damnation; Usbek is referring to the view that God may condemn men to Hell for reasons that seem unjust, such as allegiance to the wrong religion. In Letter XXXV, Usbek writes mockingly about a Muslim belief that Christians are all bound for Hell.

The argument rejecting harsh punishments is echoed in some passages concerning justice and kings. According to Letter LXXX, the Oriental habit is to punish political crimes savagely, and as a result — so Montesquieu says — the ruler's position is unsafe, rebellions being frequent. In the West, on the other hand, where punishments are moderate, the ruler is less likely to be overthrown. Letter CII returns to the point: because of the excessive severity of punishment in Persia, a subject who is out of favour has nothing to lose by treason, and 'se porte naturellement à troubler l'Etat et à conspirer contre le souverain'.

It is in Letter LXXX that we find the first example of an

overlap between the ideas of the just and the useful. The letter
begins on the question of the best government, defining it rather
obscurely: 'celui qui va à son but à moins de frais'. This is a utilitarian's remark; the suggested criterion for good government is that of
efficiency. The definition is then supported by arguments for
mildness in punishment. We must conclude that mild punishments
are more efficient, that is, of greater usefulness. But Montesquieu
also affirms that they are more just. The Asian policy of imposing
arbitrary and extreme penalties, says Usbek, 'renverse la proportion
qui doit être entre les fautes et les peines' (Letter CII), and here the
term *proportion* must mean the justness of a penalty. It is also very
close to the idea of a relationship, *rapport*, in the much-discussed
definition of justice in Letter LXXXIII: 'un rapport de convenance,
qui se trouve réellement entre deux êtres'. Montesquieu gives no
example of the 'êtres' involved, but a counter-example is easy to
find; Letter CII mentions the imposition in Persia of the death-
penalty for 'la moindre faute'. This must be an opposite both of
proportion and of *convenance*. Letter CXX criticises French laws
on abortion, which he calls 'terribles', because they prescribe the
death-penalty for an unmarried mother if she has failed to report her
pregnancy officially ('déclarer sa grossesse au Magistrat') and her
unborn child dies accidentally. As we shall see, needless waste of
life is for Montesquieu an affront not only to justice, but also to
utility.

The interconnected definitions of law and justice make a
framework for an ethics in the realms of divine, individual and
government action. The case of God is the most obscure. Apart from
the strong implication that Hell is an unjust punishment, the role of
God in Letter LXXXIII seems to be only that of conferring
transcendent status on the ideal of justice. For individual men, being
just may be a matter of exercising authority, as with God and kings;
at the end of Letter LXXXIII Usbek utters a fervent wish that he
may 'suivre toujours inviolablement cette équité que j'ai devant les
yeux', and since he is a *grand seigneur* he is presumably thinking
partly of his position of authority in society. In the same letter, just
conduct for individuals also entails not pursuing one's self-interest

at the cost of doing harm to others. This is the lesson conveyed by the fate of the first Troglodytes, in Letter XI. As for the monarch, 'la loi même', he should ensure, for the sake of stable government, that crimes are punished in proportion to the gravity of the offence. According to letter XCV, the same applies in foreign policy. The king must not declare war unless it is 'un acte de justice, dans laquelle il faut toujours que la peine soit proportionnée à la faute'.

Letter CII is the first of three letters about monarchy which develop into a discussion of delicate political topics, treason, assassination and revolution. Letter CIII, based on a contemporary event in Persia, notes that, because of the lack of any bond between an Asian ruler and his people, the assassin of the ruler can take his place without public disturbance. Turning to English history, Letter CIV alludes to events that were less recent, but more significant: the overthrow of Charles I and then of James II had had an enormous impact in France, where James's son still maintained a court. Montesquieu's train of thought is less than crystal clear, perhaps deliberately, but he probably means to say that royal authority should not be based on power alone (as in Asia), nor on divine right, nor on the hereditary principle, but on an affective bond between ruler and subjects; the king's aim should be to 'faire vivre ses sujets heureux', and they in turn will be grateful. On this condition, it seems, his power will be 'légitime'. A concept of justice, gratitude being a people's just return for enlightened government, thus enters into the discussion of the king's right to rule, and is again combined with the utilitarian idea of the public good.

To consider God as a god of justice raises an ancient theological problem, the only one that Usbek addresses. Letter LXIX, beginning in cautious style and thus indicating that the topic will again be delicate, asks how humans can act freely if God foresees their actions. This is a difficulty if God is to make just decisions. Given His power to foresee, 'la prescience infinie de Dieu', God cannot justly reward or punish — in Heaven or Hell — since rewards and punishments can be just if, and only if, the human actions that earn them have been performed freely. But how can actions be free if God foresees them? It is a question that had often been asked, and no purely rational answer has been found. What Montesquieu does is to give priority to divine justice, rather than prescience: the assumption that God is just remains untouched, but his ability to foresee can, it seems, be discarded. 'Il laisse ordinairement à la créature la faculté d'agir ou de ne pas agir' — that is, God deliberately abandons his foreknowledge of human actions — 'pour lui laisser celle de mériter ou de démériter'. (For a detailed commentary, see *34*.)

The result, broadly speaking, should be that the virtuous go to Heaven and the wicked to Hell. However, in other letters the belief in Heaven and Hell is not taken very seriously. The virtuous Anaïs is rewarded, in Letter CXLI, by heavenly joys of a distinctly physical kind, and her wicked husband is punished while still on earth, by heavenly if not divine agency. From Letter LXXVI, which argues that the laws against suicide are 'bien injustes', it can reasonably be deduced that Usbek and Montesquieu do not believe in an afterlife. How divine justice operates in practice is therefore another unresolved question.

We can affirm with confidence, however, that when justice is seen as a religious ideal, as it is in Letters LXXXIII and LXIX, the effect is to transform religion into something approaching a moral code. Letter XLVI shows this with exceptional clarity. In three different formulations, Usbek interprets religion as a matter of actions guided by civic, family and humane values. Obedience to the law is mentioned twice, humanity twice, care for members of the family twice, charity (in a wide sense, presumably) and good citizenship once; all are treated as 'actes de religion', in that they will please God. According to the argument of Letter LXIX, they should be meritorious, meaning in theological terms that they earn salvation. In its entertaining middle section, prudently located somewhere in the East, Letter XLVI establishes a strong contrast between moral conduct of this kind and the acts of religion ordained traditionally by church authorities: trivial, but much disputed. Usbek's man at prayer has been denounced, he says, for eating rabbit-meat. Those who attack him are from other religions than the Catholic —Jewish, Islamic and Greek Orthodox — but an allusion to abstention from meat (hinted at in the reference to fish) reminds us that such observances exist in Catholic custom also. For the man at prayer, the established religions seem to be distinguished merely by the most absurd of ritual differences, 'les cérémonies', and he falls back on socially valuable moral precepts, which, we can see for ourselves, are common to all religions. If we were to follow his principles, it would not only be trivial food taboos that would be abandoned, but all religious observances, such as attendance at church, that have no moral worth in themselves; several examples, including circumcision and the Latin mass, are rapidly alluded to. Nor do the clergy have any part to play in the implied scheme of things, since they are ridiculed in the persons of the 'trois hommes' and others who threaten the man at prayer with divine displeasure. Religion seems to involve only the individual, his rules of conduct, and the deity he wants to please by observing them.

In the religious domain, then, the ideal of justice evolves towards a form of deism, religion that dispenses with a church, but retains the belief in God and emphasises moral and social precepts (for a fuller treatment, see *4*, Ch.11). But the basis of Letter XLVI is not only justice. Its satirical central section has the same utilitarian foundation as the anticlerical passages elsewhere. In Letter XLV or Letter CXXXIII, for instance, clerics seem to serve no useful purpose. Nor do the observances by which Usbek's man is troubled. Other discussions of religion, in different contexts, similarly involve a nexus of ideas or values that combine justice with what (as in Chapter 3) I shall refer to as utilitarianism, without meaning anything systematic. Utility is nowhere defined in general terms, as justice is in Letter LXXXIII. However, it is often obvious in the vocabulary employed by Montesquieu, 'utile' and 'inutile' being common evaluative terms.

Utilitarianism is especially pervasive in the discussion of depopulation. Since Montesquieu's view that the earth was depopulated will seem curious, it should be said that, although his view was quite wrong, as Goubert makes clear (*14*, pp.31–35), he had some reason for it after years of scarcity and sometimes of famine. The significance of the letters on depopulation has been variously assessed (*25*, pp.42–44; *33*). In certain respects they are the counterpart at the end of the work to the first connected series of letters, those on the Troglodytes, which have similar preoccupations. The difference in treatment reflects the development in thought that takes place during the course of the *Lettres persanes*. The history of the Troglodytes is plainly allegorical; the characters, far removed from the real world, are ideas personified, and the events are contrived, demonstrating principles in action. Usbek's reflections on depopulation keep closely to what was for him historically verifiable fact. However, the threat evoked in Letter CXIII, the annihilation of the human race through epidemics, is the same in the earlier letters; in Letter XII the Troglodytes are almost wiped out. The rest of their history is devoted to the nation's recovery. In the letters after Letter CXIII, listing a series of factors which can affect the birthrate, the assumption constantly pressed upon us is that the growth of population is to be encouraged.

These letters frequently employ the vocabulary of usefulness; on the subject of seraglios, for instance, where 'un seul homme occupe à ses plaisirs tant de sujets de l'un et de l'autre sexe [...] et les rend inutiles à la propagation de l'Espèce' (Letter CXIV). In South America, many have died in the hunt for gold and silver, 'ces métaux d'eux-mêmes absolument inutiles' (Letter CXXII). When poverty is rife (here the reference must be to France), 'à quoi sert dans un état ce nombre d'enfants, qui languissent dans la misère' (Letter CXXII). As in the satirical letters, utility comes to mean the good of society, or, even more widely, that of the human race. The effect, as we read Usbek's miniature survey of universal history, is to cast the strongest possible disapproval on everything that reduces fertility and populousness: marriage customs such as polygamy or the ban on divorce; religious customs such as monasticism or the otherworldliness ascribed to Islam (the implication for Christianity is transparent); government policies such as enforced transportation of communities or colonisation. Conversely, the marriage laws of the Romans, the Jewish belief in a messiah, the Protestant abolition of the celibacy of the clergy, among other factors, are favourable to population and therefore good.

As the illustrative cases accumulate, the scope of the letters broadens, the subject becoming economically beneficial activities in general. In Letter CXV the connection between commercial prosperity and populousness is made explicitly: 'plus il y a d'hommes dans un état, plus le commerce y fleurit; [...] plus le commerce fleurit, plus le nombre des hommes y augmente: ces deux choses s'entraident et se favorisent nécessairement'. Similarly in Letter CXXII: 'L'Espèce se multiplie dans un pays où l'abondance fournit aux enfants, sans rien diminuer de la subsistance des pères'. Whatever serves material prosperity is viewed with approval. Something resembling the work ethic emerges: slaves in ancient Rome, it appears, were 'un avantage infini' to the Republic, because they worked hard. 'Cela faisait un peuple laborieux, animait les arts et l'industrie' (this phrase means the useful arts, or crafts, and entrepreneurial ingenuity, rather than manufacturing industry as we know it). Conversely, in Letter CXX, the 'sauvages' (of North America) have a 'malheureuse aversion' for work, and thus suffer frequently from famine. In Letter CXVII the same attitude is expressed through a comparison between Catholic and Protestant countries: the former suffer from celibacy and poverty, the latter are populous and rich. A similar argument is elaborated in Letter CXXII on states that are 'soumis au pouvoir arbitraire' and those that enjoy republican government.

With greater subtlety and caution, then, the letters on depopulation point in the same direction as the Troglodyte letters: to the prospect of well-populated, industrious and materially successful societies. The discussion usually focuses on the numerous threats to this prospect, from sexual disease to enforced military service. It would be an exaggeration to say that an economic theory is implied — thought about economics was in its infancy — but the utilitarian basis for such a theory is present: a consistent pattern of values giving priority to anything that favours economic progress. Whatever runs counter to this objective, however venerable, is criticised. One of the most vehement passages in the *Lettres persanes* attacks monasticism, 'ce métier de continence', which according to Letter CXVII will eventually cause the Catholic religion to disappear entirely; and in Letter CXXII the terms in which 'pouvoir arbitraire' is described suggest that Montesquieu is thinking of the huge expenses of the French court, as he is in the imaginary royal decree of Letter CXXIV.

The same belief in what we have come to call material progress is often to be found outside the depopulation letters. In Letter LVIII it is mixed with satire, Rica pretending to admire some questionable ways of earning a living in Paris, such as teaching foreign languages without knowing them; but he also says that the citizens' incomes 'ne consistent qu'en esprit et qu'en industrie', like the enterprising Roman slaves of Letter CXV, and he ends by surrendering completely to the *douceur de vivre* in 'cette ville enchanteresse'. In the more serious Letter CVI Usbek quashes Rhédi's doubts about the value of 'les arts', which here comes to mean technical advance, and makes the same point as Rica about Paris: 'on n'y voit que travail et industrie'. (He is also worried already about depopulation; if the basic agricultural skills alone were known, 'le peuple dépérirait tous les jours'.) In Letter XCVII, advances in pure science are hailed as proof of Western superiority over the East, with a strong hint that science is more valuable than holy books. Here the motive for Usbek's admiration is as much utilitarian as intellectual, the results of scientific advance often being practical: rainfall can be measured — an important consideration for agriculturalists — and ships can be designed to sail more efficiently.

In the early eighteenth century, arguments such as those in Letter CVI would have been seen as contributing to the 'querelle du luxe', a debate about the rights and wrongs of material affluence. Montesquieu is on the side of those who, like Voltaire in *Le Mondain* of 1736 and Bernard Mandeville in his *Fable of the Bees* (1723), subtitled 'Private Vices, Publick Benefits', defend the enjoyment of luxury on the grounds that it requires and encourages industry and commerce. In Letter CVI, for instance, Usbek affirms: 'Pour qu'un homme vive délicieusement, il faut que cent autres travaillent sans relâche'. This is not a criticism of inequalities in the social order, but an assertion of their advantages, since the hundred workers benefit also.

When utilitarian arguments almost become a defence of élitist hedonism, as in this passage, we seem to have come a long way from the simplicities of Troglodyte cooperation and ideals of divine and human justice. If utilitarianism in public policy is the principle that citizens should prosper, we might expect Montesquieu's other ideal, that of justice, to demand that they should prosper more or less equally. And in Letter CXXII we find, indeed, that one of the advantages of republican government is 'l'égalité même des citoyens, qui produit ordinairement de l'égalité dans les fortunes'. Since this is the last of the series on depopulation, and includes a passage deploring poverty in France, its tentative advocacy of equality in wealth should perhaps be given more weight than the suggestion in Letter CVI that riches for the few are of benefit for the many. However, too little is said to draw firm conclusions.

To conclude, as I think we must, that the principles of justice and the diffuse utilitarianism which are both prominent in the work are not knitted together into a clear philosophy, consistently applied, may disappoint those for whom clarity and consistency are paramount, but Montesquieu was not among those thinkers who want to fit everything into a system. The categories of his thought are capacious and not always well defined, his interests ranging over too many facets of human behaviour for a narrowly systematic approach to be either possible or desirable. The furthest we can go by way of generalisation is to relate the values of justice and utility to the point of view from which the satirical letters are written, that of concern for the public good. Both values reflect this concern, utility the more obviously, since what is in question is the degree of usefulness for society. Justice is the ideal that should order the transactions of authority with individuals; in this area the subject most discussed in the *Lettres persanes* is the relation between crime and punishment, and the fundamental argument is that the welfare of society, as well as moral idealism, is best served by moderation in the punishment of offenders. Usbek's outlook in abstract discussion is much the same as that implied in Rica's satire, although the subjects of their theorising and mockery are usually diverse.

6. Narratives: Usbek's Seraglio and Two Short Stories

The importance of the early letters about Usbek's seraglio is as much documentary as narrative; placed as they are before the Persians' visit to France, they create a background of systematic oppression. The seraglio, regarded by Usbek as a protection for his wives' virtue, acts for the reader as an image of captivity which gives point to the observations about the freedom of women in France. The narrative component becomes apparent gradually, its full significance being manifest only at the close. It is also fragmented, several different stories about the seraglio being recounted discontinuously, because of the epistolary form. Take the career of Zélide, one of the slaves: from the complaints made by Zéphis in Letter IV it seems that one of the eunuchs suspects a lesbian relationship between her and Zélide. The end of Letter XX tells us that, having been moved and now serving Zachi instead, Zélide is the object of the same accusation from another slave. Finally, Letter LIII, from Zélis, is a request that Zélide — again moved — should be allowed to marry a eunuch. If we take the hints (confirmed in Letter CXLVII) and regard the lesbianism as proved, Zélide's sexuality may explain the bizarre idea of the marriage. We can also infer that Zélis, by contrast, does not resort to lesbianism, and so at the time of Letter LIII is still faithful to Usbek.

Not all the associated narratives have to be pieced together in this way. Roxane's story is told in a comparatively straightforward manner, given the constraints of narration by letter. When combined, the narratives about the wives as individuals, and the letters (mainly from the eunuchs) about events in the life of the seraglio, form a single main story. Its subject is the dissolution of the seraglio, a social unit made up of wives, eunuchs and slaves, with an absent master. As Usbek approaches Europe, Letters XX and XXII convey the situation: infringements of the rules of chastity, a eunuch savagely punished, and stricter surveillance. In Letter XLVII Zachi's appeal for Usbek to return is due to her love for him, or so it seems, but in Letter LXIV the same appeal is made by the Chef des Eunuques Noirs because of difficulties in maintaining discipline. According to him, Usbek is too kind to his wives (and no doubt to Pharan, the slave who had been threatened with castration in Letter XLI). Usbek disregards the eunuch's advice. Letter LXV, to his wives, is no more than a mild reprimand, of the same kind as Letter XX. At this stage, his moderation apparently achieves its purpose. Although the chief black eunuch (a character with several titles: Le chef des eunuques noirs, Le premier eunuque noir, Le grand eunuque noir must all be the same person) writes again in Letter LXXIX, he does not mention indiscipline. Letter XCVI ends with another request that Usbek should return, but in less anxious terms than Letter LXIV. Nearly five years after Usbek's departure, the Persian marriage system is still functioning effectively.

Eighteen months later, the situation has deteriorated sharply, as the Grand Eunuque reports in Letter CXLVII. From here until the end, the news from the seraglio is consistently bad. The narrative mode also changes markedly, the letters being grouped in one sequence instead of following the order of the date of writing. The effect is twofold; continuity is enhanced, and communication by letter itself comes to be important in the plot. In outline the plot is simple. Letter CXLVII lists new offences against discipline: Zélis has deliberately neglected the precautions against being seen unveiled in public (scrupulously observed long before, according to Letter XLVII); and Zachi has reverted to her lesbian habits. In Letter CXLVIII, Usbek reverses his previous policy of moderation, and commands 'les punitions et les châtiments'. He seems not to consider returning to Persia himself. The death of the chief eunuch, and his replacement by the foolish and possibly corrupt Narsit, prevent Usbek's orders being carried out before worse disasters befall. Solim discovers that Roxane's fidelity was faked (Letter CLIX), and in the final collapse of the seraglio her lover is killed and she takes poison, despatching the eunuchs as well (Letter CLXI:

'mon ombre s'envole bien accompagnée; je viens d'envoyer devant moi ces gardiens sacrilèges, qui ont répandu le plus beau sang du Monde'). By comparing Letter CLX and Letter CLXI, we can infer that she has killed the eunuchs only just before Solim fulfils his plans to execute her and the other erring wives.

Roxane's private rebellion has a retroactive effect on previous letters, especially Letter XXVI, which read on its own is a tribute to womanly chastity of the Persian kind. The convention was (in Chardin's account) that it was unseemly for a new wife to accept too quickly the advances of her husband: accordingly, the reluctance of Roxane had seemed to Usbek to prove that she was chaste. However, when read in the light of Letter CLXI, Usbek's previous remarks about her unwillingness come to seem the blind expression of male complacency. Failing to perceive that her repugnance was all too genuine, he recalls that he made her surrender only by force, or in other words that he raped her ('vous défendîtes jusqu'à la dernière extrémité une virginité mourante'). In the last letter, Roxane rewrites the incident: 'Si tu m'avais bien connue, tu y aurais trouvé toute la violence de la haine'.

The ending also alters our perceptions of Zélis, although in her case there are extraneous considerations. Zélis stands out because she is a mother (the lack of other children in the seraglio bears out Letter CXIV's arguments about polygamy). Discussing her daughter's upbringing in Letter LXII, her language is that of feminine submissiveness ('une éducation sainte dans les sacrés murs où la pudeur habite'). At the end of her letter, the phrasing becomes a shade equivocal: what does 'j'ai goûté ici mille plaisirs que tu ne connais pas' mean? The word 'imagination' in the following sentence, while not entirely dispelling the ambiguity, implies that she had referred merely to daydreams of pleasure. The next letter from her, Letter LXX, and the reply from Usbek, show them to be on good terms, as they agree about the injustice suffered by the daughter of Soliman (both seeming more concerned with the plight of the parent than that of the daughter).

In the published text, the next reference to Zélis is in Letter CXLVII, and is unexpected, since we are now told that she has offended against *pudeur* by being seen 'presque à visage découvert devant tout le peuple'. Her behaviour becomes more explicable if we take into account one of the letters left in manuscript form (*1*, p.417; *2*, p.344). The information that Usbek discloses here is startling, for he writes: 'Vous demandez devant le juge votre séparation'. His response is to reimpose the *éducation* which, he says, she has forgotten, and he finally threatens to kill her if she persists in her request. The letter's date is significant: 1 February 1718. Letter CXLVIII, Usbek's reply to the eunuch's report of the wives' offences, including that of Zélis, is dated 11 February 1718.

In other words, in an episode later abandoned, Montesquieu must have intended the first sign of the wives' rebellion to be Zélis's request for a divorce; the letter left in manuscript would have been placed before Letter CXLVII, which begins the final sequence in the published text. This sheds new light on Usbek's suspicions of Zélis, mentioned at the end of Letter CXLVIII. To judge from the published text alone, he has little reason to suspect her, and when Roxane is discovered to be guilty, in Letter CLIX, Zélis seems to be exonerated. But if we can accept that she had sought a judicial separation, other references to her become more meaningful. It is she as well as Roxane who goes to stay in the country, according to the gullible Narsit in Letter CLII; in the preceding letter, Solim reports that two men are said to have been hiding in one of Usbek's houses, which must be the same as the one visited by the two apparently virtuous wives. The evidence is not conclusive, for the hints and allusions do not fit together in as clear a pattern as in Roxane's story, but the discarded letter about Zélis strongly suggests that she too, the mother of Usbek's daughter, was meant finally to be wholly disloyal to him. It can also be deduced that there was some degree of collaboration between her and Roxane, which adds to the fictional demonstration that the Persian method of ensuring love by frustration and discipline is bound to prove inadequate.

Without any doubt, the events of the ending are intended to produce sympathy for the wives, especially Roxane, who is willing to suffer death for the sake of her prohibited love. About the ultimate cause and the further significance of the ending there is much more room for discussion. Vartanian (*30*) argues that the meaning is essentially political, and concerns freedom and oppression. As regards causes, the course of the plot on its own suggests that, in personal rather than philosophical terms, the seraglio's downfall is due mainly to the simple fact of Usbek's prolonged absence. This is the view taken by the eunuch in Letter XCVI, urging Usbek to return. Usbek has authority, it seems, not only because he can decree punishments, but partly also because he can satisfy the wives sexually: 'Viens adoucir des passions désespérées; viens ôter tout prétexte de faillir'. The eunuch's argument is supported by the situation at the time, since the previous troubles in the seraglio have apparently been pacified.

When the troubles recur, the other factor that I have mentioned comes into play: the breakdown of communication by letter. Considered in terms of narrative technique, the last group of letters is highly interesting. They form part of the story themselves, in the manner brilliantly elaborated in *Les Liaisons dangereuses*. Montesquieu does not develop the technique as far as Laclos, but he applies the central principle: that when characters take action by letter, as Usbek has to, the physical conditions of communication can become part of the plot. Ironically, Usbek in Letter XXVII had been impressed with the reliability of the letter service between Paris and Ispahan. Yet the delay in the letter's arrival — up to five months is required — is an important element in the plot. Assuming that Usbek replies at once to the letters from Persia, it must be February 1718 when the first of the final sequence, sent from Persia in September 1717, arrives in Paris. Usbek's reply ordering punishment, Letter CXLVIII, arrives in Persia in July 1718, but is left unopened (Letter CXLIX). He does not know this until December. He sends new orders to reimpose discipline, but they are lost. Narsit says that the loss is due to misfortune, the letter having been stolen from a slave (Letter CLII); Solim in Letter CLI implies that the theft might have been part of a conspiracy. Only in March 1720 does the harsh and loyal Solim receive and act on the orders that Usbek had originally issued in February 1718, in response to a report about the situation five months earlier. The wives have therefore enjoyed about two and a half years of impunity, and even after the reimposition of duty Roxane continues to see her lover until Solim discovers them together.

That the final collapse of the seraglio is in part due to the vicissitudes of communication might suggest that the failure is largely due to chance. But the underlying cause is time, at least as regards most of the wives. Nothing would have altered Roxane's attitude, but initially the other wives are not hostile to their husband. The source of their disaffection is partly Usbek's absence, but also the fact that it lasts so long. Here the two consecutive letters, Letter LXIV and LXV, dated May and October 1714, are crucial: advised to act severely, Usbek does the opposite and contents himself with an appeal to his wives' good nature (though he supports his appeal with a threat). Since his mild policy appears to succeed, he seems justified in extending his absence in France, but it must be because of the length of his stay that the later disorders occur, and prove to be intractable. Pursuing causes further still, we find in letter CLV two motives for him not to return home: the dangers he faces from his enemies in Persia, and Rica's disinclination to leave France. Usbek himself claims in this letter to find France 'un climat barbare'. Since he has travelled there for the sake of study, we must presume that anything else he finds is at best indifferent to him, if not unpleasant.

A more abstract interpretation would be that it is necessary for Usbek to remain away from the seraglio simply because the letter-series cannot continue unless he does so. As has often been observed, fiction in letter form requires the protagonists to be at a distance from one another. On this view, Usbek's absence has no real causal or psychological significance, but is a structural necessity, a condition without which there would be no story to read. The argument seems to me partly correct, but does not explain why the events that occur in the story should end as they do; even after all the delays, a happier ending would not be impossible within the epistolary convention. The form of the story affects it only up to a point; its causality depends mainly on psychological and moral norms. However it is told, the seraglio oppresses the wives, and it is

Usbek's belief in the system and his authority that lead to the disastrous ending. Even in his despairing Letter CLV, he still expects to receive his wives' 'empressements' when he finally returns to them, although he has already commanded them to be punished. Whatever the effect of French civilisation on him may be, it does not alter his attitude to marriage.

After the grim and stormy atmosphere of Usbek's seraglio, it is a relief to turn to two lighter Oriental stories, in Letter LXVII and Letter CXLI. It is not that they are free from difficulties; Ibben's story of his friend Aphéridon's love for Astarté ends with the pair living happily ever after, with their daughter, but they happen to be brother and sister. This makes Letter LXVII one of the most remarkable of the series, not to speak of eighteenth-century fiction generally. It has an obvious message: that what is usually called incest (the word is avoided) can produce a marriage that is not only happy, but ideal. The tone is utterly serious throughout, the style resembling that of the Troglodyte letters, full of expressions of heroic sentiment, probably modelled on the example of Fénelon's *Télémaque*, of 1699, which Montesquieu much admired (like most others in the eighteenth century).

One possible explanation is biographical. Vantuch (*29*) has argued persuasively that the story reflects Montesquieu's feelings for his sister Thérèse, slightly younger than he, who became a nun. Astarté is two years younger than Aphéridon, their story begins with their close affection during childhood, and she is later separated from him by marriage to a eunuch — Letter CXVII calls both monks and nuns 'eunuques' — in a religion which forbids siblings to marry. That Aphéridon surmounts all obstacles and rescues Astarté from her captive state could therefore be unconscious wish-fulfilment, taking a fictional form because of the taboo on brother-sister marriage. The religious aspect of the story could have originated in the situation between Montesquieu and his real wife, Jeanne de Lartigue, whom he seems not to have loved, but who came from a Huguenot family and never gave up her Protestant convictions (*8*, p.61; *25*, p.14): the important argument between Aphéridon and Astarté, who is a reluctant convert to Islam, resembles those between Catholics and Protestants since the Reformation. Aphéridon says that his religion, that of the Gabars or Ghebers, is older than Islam, and Astarté that her new religion is 'plus pure'. The claim of purity, the worship of God alone, not idols, was constantly made by the Reformers; they accused the Catholics of image-worship, which is close to Astarté's statement that the Gabars worship created things.

Allowing for some adjustments, then, there is enough in the biographical background to make Vantuch's central contention plausible, though perhaps the usual reservation should be made about psychoanalytical interpretations, that they are not susceptible of positive proof. But even if we set the question of the story's origins to one side, we still need to account for its frank treatment of its subject. That the hero and heroine are brother and sister, that they are prevented from marrying because of religious prohibitions, and that when married they are absolutely devoted to each other, are all heavily emphasised. Montesquieu even writes of 'notre impatience amoureuse'. The other values embodied in the marriage can be inferred from what Aphéridon says about Astarté's enforced marriage to the eunuch: 'vous avez perdu votre liberté, votre bonheur et cette précieuse égalité qui fait l'honneur de votre sexe'. Of Aphéridon, Ibben says that 'il y a plus d'héroïsme dans son cœur que dans celui des plus grands monarques', and his conduct is exemplary throughout. The suggestion that brothers should be allowed to marry their sisters is impossible to avoid, but I also find it hard to believe that it is meant as a recommendation.

We might perhaps resolve the dilemma by saying that the story is meant as an example of exoticism, bringing to the notice of Europeans the curious customs of the East, except that Montesquieu's sources (2, p.139) must have made it clear to him that sibling marriage in the Gabar religion belonged to the distant past, if indeed it had occurred at all. My only contribution to the discussion is to point to the frequent references to unity, 'l'union', a recurrent motif in the passages about the lovers' feelings for each other. 'Ces alliances saintes', says Aphéridon of sibling marriages, are true images of 'l'union déjà formée par la nature'. Before the marriage ceremony, the assertion is more emphatic still: 'Que cette union est sainte! [...] La Nature nous avait unis; notre sainte loi va nous unir encore'. In his final remarks, Aphéridon says that he enjoys 'la plus aimable et la plus douce société du monde: l'union règne dans ma famille'. Unity seems to be the highest of values, and to be natural within the family. It is also dear to the Troglodytes, who regard themselves as 'une seule famille' (Letter XII); and in Usbek's vision of the end of religious conflict in Letter XXXV, he imagines all men at one, 'sous le même étendard'. It would seem, then, that Letter LXVII carries over into marriage an ideal of emotional unity derived from family relationships; but it remains something of a puzzle.

The short story in Letter CXLI contains similar elements, for its plot involves a seraglio, religion, and fantasy, but in this case the fantasy is largely for entertainment, and does not call for extended commentary. The plot is a kind of reversal of the main seraglio story. Anaïs makes a direct protest to her barbarous husband and is stabbed to death. Presumably by the operation of divine justice in a pseudo-Islamic guise, her heroic virtue is rewarded by the type of happiness she had been denied in the seraglio, constantly renewed sexual ecstasies, relieved by less active pleasures during the day. (The prevalent belief at the time was that the Muslim paradise was one of exclusively sensual delights; in describing them, Montesquieu was almost certainly making a point about the Christian view of Heaven, which he mocks by implication in Letter CXXV.) The pleasure of the story, however, lies in the revenge that Anaïs organises for the benefit of her former companions in misery. It is recounted with many comic ambiguities on the subject of sex. The implied view of women is not elevated: it seems that sharing a man will make the wives entirely happy, provided that his resources are equal to his responsibilities.

The situation in Ibrahim's seraglio, when he has been removed, is too close to that of Usbek and his wives for us not to form inferences about them also. It is not just that the story in Letter CXLI, with its male intruder into the seraglio, anticipates what is to be discovered in Letter CLIX (their dates are almost the same), but that the parallel situations have opposite sequels. While Usbek is absent his frustrated wives are kept under control by severe discipline, which eventually fails; while Ibrahim is absent, his wives, sexually satisfied, are fond and faithful. They also produce large numbers of children, in strong contrast to the one daughter in Usbek's seraglio. If the element of fantasy were not so pronounced, we might suppose the message to be that Usbek could have made polygamy acceptable and productive by being on the spot to make love to his wives, but the unreality of the story is such as to imply that polygamy can work only in totally imaginary circumstances, when the husband has more-than-human virility. This exactly complements what Usbek himself has said in Letter CXIV, and so makes another condemnation of the Asian type of marriage. Although Usbek is the main character in the book he cannot have been meant, in his role as husband (as opposed to that of thinker), as an admirable figure. At best his fate might arouse compassion, his suffering being powerfully depicted in his last letter, but all the narratives in the *Lettres persanes* go to show that the polygamous form of marriage to which he clings is inhumane and futile.

7. Endings and Conclusions

From the beginning, Montesquieu has occasionally devoted letters
to a group of subjects which include books, study, and the quirks of
intellectuals. Towards the end of the Persians' stay, from Letter
CVIII, on book reviews, these subjects become much more
prominent. Letter CIX is on the Sorbonne and Letter CXI on
memoirs of the Fronde; after the letters on depopulation and others
mainly about current events, Letter CXXVIII mildly satirises the
café society of intellectuals, and Letter CXXX, more scathingly, the
meetings of *nouvellistes*, semi-professional gatherers of news whose
activities anticipated those of today's agencies. The most important
of the letters dealing with the world of learning are the series on the
library that Rica visits, Letters CXXXIII to CXXXVII, and of these
Letter CXXXVI stands out. It is closely related to Letter CXXXI by
its subjects, political history and liberty. Finally Letters CXLII,
CXLIII and CXLV, all of which are long and complicated and
contain letters-within-letters, concern among other things the follies
of an antiquarian, the power of the written word, and the position of
the intellectual in society. The general subject is the proper use of
human reason.

Most of these letters are from Rica, and it is his caustic tone
that is predominant, though less so than in the early satire on social
life. Intellectual satire is a less common variety. Its basis here is still
the same, the utilitarian outlook, which mocks at those who use
their minds in trivial and pointless ways. Letter CIX describes the
Sorbonne as the kind of place that spends its time on futile debates
about the ancient world, like the café wits of Letter XXXVI. We
have already been told in Letter LXXIII that the other great intellectual institution, the Académie française, is no wiser: its attention is
taken up with finding new ways of telling Louis XIV how great he
is. The ridiculous antiquarian in Letter CXLII squanders money and

energy on empty relics of the distant past. In Letter CXXVIII a
mathematician makes a similar point about translations (from
ancient languages: the Persians are relentless modernists). He
himself, however, illustrates *déformation professionnelle* above all;
I can see no suggestion that mathematics is a waste of time.

Elsewhere, utility of a different variety is at issue: the value
and efficacy of printed writings. Having travelled far in order to
study, the Persians have the right to be critical about what they read,
and criticise with vigour. In Letter LXVI, Usbek is irritated by a
book that promised 'la science universelle', but gave him only a
headache. Letter CVIII considers without indulgence the value of
periodicals containing book reviews, which at the time were often
no more than summaries. Usbek adds some tart observations about
authors who write for their own benefit rather than the reader's. The
satire goes into the fantastic mode in Letter CXI, which is itself
about a kind of satire, the 'Mazarinades' of the Fronde, songs and
sketches attacking the Cardinal; the general whose letter Usbek
passes on to us relies on the satirical attacks for victory, 'quoique
nos troupes aient été repoussées avec perte'. In Letter CXLIII, Rica
launches into an elaborate joke depending on the same idea, the
physical effectiveness of words. Taking his cue from superstitions
about the power of talismans, 'l'arrangement de certaines lettres',
Rica first records the soporific effect of books by a little-known
Jesuit writer, Caussin, selected for no clear reason except that
Montesquieu must have found him extremely boring, and follows up
with a series of burlesque medical prescriptions. Pages from various
books have emetic or laxative powers, it seems, when infused with
water. Jesuits again come off badly, but so too do poets and
Aristotle. The last prescription, a cure for love-sickness by means of
pornography, is decently clothed in Latin.

Such back-handed tributes to the value of books are designed
almost entirely for entertainment, of a rather sophisticated kind,
although they also tell us that the books concerned are worthless.
With less brutality, but still sharply, the four letters about the library
that Rica visits undertake a universal review of categories of book:
religious; learned and scientific; historical; and literary. The

introductory Letter CXXXIII gives us a symbol of uselessness in the person of a greedy monk whom I have mentioned before; he offers Rica no help, making an unfortunate contrast with the librarian, whose assistance later is invaluable. The monk calls him 'un homme qui n'est bon à rien'.

The librarian himself judges books in the same way, by their function, but sensibly. He notes above all their effects on the reader or their success in achieving their purpose. Books on alchemy, anatomy, and occult science are therefore condemned, in Letter CXXXV (though by another ironic twist Rica defends the astrologers; this is in order to attack the financial 'algèbre' of Law's 'Système'). Letter CXXXIV on religious books contains the librarian's only directly favourable judgement: books on *morale* are useful. The commentators on Holy Writ, by contrast, defeat their own purpose, substituting their own doctrines for those contained in the Bible; mystics turn piety into 'délire'; and casuists, supposedly deciding moral issues, teach immorality instead.

On literature, the utilitarian attitude may seem unduly narrow-minded. The business of poets, we are told, is 'de mettre des entraves au bon sens et d'accabler la raison sous des agréments', which implies that in Montesquieu's view literary discourse should be reasonable and nothing else. He excludes the possibility that the irrational in poetry, or in imaginative literature generally, might be of value. The authors of *romans* (here meaning romances of chivalry in the medieval style) are also 'des espèces de poètes', their fault being that they put exaggeration in the place of realism. The early eighteenth century is often regarded as an unpoetic era, and Montesquieu's utilitarian insistence that discourse should communicate clearly may help to explain why. Dramatic poets are more favourably treated (even someone entirely out of sympathy with poetry could hardly ignore the claims of Corneille, Molière and Racine), but all that the librarian can find to say about them is that their plays are moving.

He has a slightly fuller opinion about epigrams, his comment emphasising the violence of the effect on their victims: 'une plaie profonde et inaccessible aux remèdes'. Since epigrammatic

literature is close to satire, we can infer that Montesquieu was aware
of satire's aggression and destructiveness. These are the character-
istics implied in the remarks about the 'Mazarinades' in Letter CXI.
Nothing suggests that he considers his own writing to belong to the
same satirical category as epigrams or pamphlets against Mazarin
— as I have said, the satire in the *Lettres persanes* is mild — but
since the librarian is almost exclusively interested in the effects of
literature, and of writing generally, we can conclude at least that in
Montesquieu's view the printed word was essentially active, a
method of influencing readers in one way or another. For instance,
the story in Letter CXLI is told by the learned Zuléma, who is said
to have 'un certain caractère d'esprit enjoué qui laissait à peine
deviner si elle voulait amuser ceux à qui elle parlait, ou les
instruire'. To entertain and instruct was in Montesquieu's time the
constantly repeated formulation of the double purpose of literature,
and through it we can grasp how the nature of his writing in the
Lettres persanes corresponds to its utilitarian outlook. To instruct is
manifestly to serve a useful purpose, and to be instructed (like the
Persians) is to be usefully employed, especially if the content of the
instruction itself relates to various types of utility, social and
intellectual. The entertainment is subordinate, a means rather than
an end (although in Zuléma's tale it is indeed hard to tell which aim
is dominant); fiction and satire entertain us — assuming that they
are effective — while also teaching us what is and is not valuable,
both personally and socially.

When the librarian comes to history, he changes his point of
view, and speaks as a student, inquiring what can be learned from
the books. In other words, historical writing is the one kind that is
unequivocally useful. However, he is not interested merely in factual
information. What history teaches appears from Letter CXXXVI to
go well beyond the utilitarian: the lesson is a political one, the value
of freedom. With great consistency, as the librarian guides Rica
through the late centuries of Roman history to the Holy Roman
Empire, then to France, Spain, England, and other states of modern
Europe, he notes the extent to which freedom is possessed by the
various nations, allotting criticism or praise according as they have

lost or preserved it. England and the republics, mainly Holland and Switzerland, receive the greatest approval. *Liberté* has both its external and internal senses: independence from neighbouring powers, but also from governmental absolutism. It is the latter that is meant in an important remark about the 'peuples barbares', the mainly Germanic tribes who founded the European nations. In modern times, says the librarian, these states have been 'soumis pour la plupart à une puissance absolue', and have lost 'cette douce liberté si conforme à la raison, à l'humanité et à la nature'.

This open proclamation of belief in freedom makes Letter CXXVI almost a political manifesto. Montesquieu is hardly less explicit in his admiration for states that have rejected or rebelled against monarchy. In the passage on France, the metaphorical language about raging torrents is a thin disguise for the message that the monarchy has become too powerful. A nearby letter, Letter CXXXI, contains a further development of the same arguments. In it Rhédi writes of what he has learned from history about republics; for him they are an opposite to despotism, and from his examples it can be inferred that they are states in which at least some of the citizens, from a few leading families to the (male) population at large, have a part in the government. The implied definitions were to be clarified in the famous typology of governments in the *Esprit des lois* (II, i): 'le gouvernement républicain est celui où le peuple en corps, ou seulement une partie du peuple, a la souveraine puissance; le monarchique, celui où un seul gouverne, mais par des lois fixes et établies; au lieu que, dans le despotique, un seul, sans loi et sans règle, entraîne tout par sa volonté et ses caprices'. The contrast that Rhédi makes, revealing the same preoccupations as the librarian, is between Eastern absolutism ('les peuples d'Asie [...] soumis à la volonté d'un seul') and Western republicanism, which depends on 'l'amour de la liberté, la haine des rois'.

The interest in these letters is not only that they express admiration for freedom generally, which is in conformity with Roxane's tragic tirade in Letter CLXI; they also raise an issue of more limited but topical significance, the powers of the French monarchy. In a period when the question of origins was crucial, the situation of the monarchy at its beginnings in the early Middle Ages was thought to have determined its rights and prerogatives in perpetuity. Rhédi avoids mentioning the Franks, the Germanic tribe whose great king Clovis was, by tradition, the founder of the French monarchy, but all his arguments bear on the question of the powers of the Germanic kings, and hence of the modern monarch. He greatly restricts their powers: royal authority was shared with the nobles, who had to consent to declarations of war; taxes were not levied for the benefit of the king; and 'les lois étaient faites dans les assemblées de la Nation', not by the king in council. Rhédi even mentions that some tribes, the Goths and Vandals, deposed their kings. The customs he lists formed, according to him, 'le principe fondamental de tous ces états qui se formèrent du débris de l'Empire romain', which must include France; if the relevance to France was not apparent in Rhédi's letter, it could be established from a passage in Letter CXXXVI about the peoples who 'fondèrent tous les royaumes que vous voyez à présent en Europe'.

Liberté, then, should be understood in the context of opposed contemporary attitudes in politics. Against the *thèse nobiliaire* which defended the prerogatives of the nobility, the *thèse royale* (put forward by Voltaire among others) asserted those of the king. The arguments in Letter CXXXI are a clear but moderate expression of the *thèse nobiliaire*, supporting a division of governmental authority between king and nobility, which would end royal absolutism. This, according to Letter CXXXVI, has reached an extreme, 'son dernier période'. The reference must be to Louis XIV.

By interpreting the two letters about history as combative reflections on the relative powers of king and nobles, I do not mean to diminish their scope as assertions of an ideal of political liberty. It remains an ideal, even if its expression is adapted to the particular circumstances of debate in Montesquieu's time. Whether the belief in political freedom should be interpreted as revolutionary is another question. Because the Enlightenment was followed by the Revolution, it has been argued ever since that the one was a cause of the other. As regards the *Lettres persanes*, the argument can be illustrated by a remark on the work's revolutionary tendencies made by Paul Valéry, who wrote in a preface to it that the Persians' naïve surprise disturbs confidence in the established order, adding: 'C'est aussi prophétiser le retour à quelque désordre; et même faire un peu plus que de le prédire'. Against Valéry's opinion, which seems to me to be exaggerated, we could point to Letter CXXIX. A writer who, like Montesquieu here, can speak of 'les désordres inséparables des changements', and can say that, on the rare occasions when laws need to be changed, 'il n'y faut toucher que d'une main tremblante', seems unlikely to advocate a complete upheaval in government. The considerations taken from history in Letter CXXXI and CXXXVI suggest that the monarchy has extended its power too far at the expense of the rest of the nation, and that the balance should be redressed, but not that the monarchy should be abolished.

However, as we have seen, Letter CIV advances the idea that, if a ruler oppresses his people, they no longer have the duty of obedience. This allows for the possibility of revolution in circumstances of tyranny. If revolution means the overthrow of tyrants, then, Montesquieu's views could be said to be revolutionary in tendency. Yet he is keenly aware of the differences between nations, and his expressed admiration for the English, Dutch and Swiss republics is not the same as a recommendation that the type of government that succeeds there should be adopted by all states; republican government is admired in its particular historical setting, not set up as an Utopian ideal that is to be imposed universally.

To return to the uses of learning: Letter CXXXVI shows Rica the utility of history, while the similar reflections in Letter CXXXI are the result of Rhédi's own investigations, spurred on by his curiosity about European republics. Both letters exemplify the kind of lesson that the Persians can learn only by coming to Europe; Rhédi says that 'la plupart des Asiatiques n'ont pas seulement d'idée de cette sorte de gouvernement'. Looking back, it is remarkable how often previous letters have been framed as lessons, either from the French whom Rica and Usbek meet, as in Letters XLVIII or LXXXIX, or from themselves when answering questions put to them by correspondents, Mirza or Rhédi. It is Rhédi who outlines an ambitious programme of study in Letter XXXI, receives from Usbek several important letters on religion, is assailed by doubts about the value of what he is learning in Letter CV, and in Letter CXII, led by his reading to worry about depopulation, calls forth Usbek's disquisition on it.

The fiction that it is Persians who are learning, arguing and reflecting is transparent, of course, and is in a sense negligible; we rightly talk of 'Montesquieu's views on depopulation', not Usbek's. Yet the metaphor of a journey for the sake of enlightenment has its significance. To quote Rhédi again: 'je sors des nuages qui couvraient mes yeux dans le pays de ma naissance' (Letter XXXI). Since Usbek and Rica come to France for instruction, the story of their sojourn there is largely the story of their intellectual development. As I have said, Rica is the more receptive to French ways. He is prepared to wear French dress in Letter XXX, and is more appreciative of the freedom enjoyed by French women. On this point Usbek remains unyielding, but he is tolerant of religious differences. In Letter LXIII, Rica tells Usbek that he has become almost completely assimilated into French society: 'Mon esprit perd insensiblement tout ce qui lui reste d'asiatique, et se plie sans effort aux mœurs européennes'. Rica speaks like this because of the advantages for getting to know women, but even if we suspect his motives the result is not in doubt. The same letter suggests that Usbek too finds advantages in the social life of France; Rica, noting that his friend has been away visiting longer than expected, explains it by the opportunities for intellectual discussion: 'Il est vrai que tu es dans une maison charmante, que tu y trouves une société qui te convient, que tu y raisonnes tout à ton aise'.

The process of integration into French life has taken two years. Henceforth, when beginning their letters, both habitually allude to the fact that they are in a foreign land (when they do not, as in Letter XCIV, the effect is faintly unusual), but their concerns are usually those of their adoptive country, Rica admiring the institution of the Invalides almost as if he were a Frenchman. There remains a slight difference between the two; when in Letter CLV Usbek resigns himself to the necessity of returning to Persia, his remarks about France are hostile, and he blames Rica for wanting to stay; 'il m'attache ici par mille prétextes; il semble qu'il ait oublié sa patrie'. By the end of their stay, then, Rica and Usbek have become more French than Persian, though Usbek's personal situation makes him wish to leave. They continue to profess themselves Muslims, but their loyalty to Islam wears rather thin. Although in Letter CXXIII Usbek grieves over the defeats of the Turks, in Letter CXLII Rica describes his habit of wearing Koranic amulets as mere credulity.

However, to define their attitude only in terms of nationality is incomplete. They develop less into Frenchmen than into internationalists, rising above distinctions of country, and taking the view of a 'citizen of the world', in Oliver Goldsmith's phrase. This is especially noticeable in the enquiry into depopulation, the scope of which is universal. Usbek's last sentence comments on the loss of inhabitants in France, but he then asks: 'que sera-ce dans les autres états?', extending his concern world-wide. The same is true of other passages, such as those on international law in Letters XCIV and XCV, or on 'les arts' in Letters CV and CVI. Usbek lays down principles that apply to any government in any country, his Persian background and acquired French culture giving his reflections greater force than if they had been presented only from the French point of view. By imperceptible stages we are made to share in an attitude that transcends boundaries of nationality and religion. Ibben adds an emotional dimension to the process when he says in Letter LXVII that 'Le coeur est citoyen de tous les pays', and denies that differences of nationality should affect friendship or compassion.

Even so, national distinctions are never neglected. On political freedom, I have argued that in the *Lettres persanes* it is both an ideal to be generally admired and a characteristic of particular countries. So too with the values of justice and moderation. The Persians see them as universally applicable, but also as being typical of Europe rather than the East. Here the question raised at the end of Chapter 2, about the degree of national differences, becomes relevant. The commonly-held view that the *Lettres persanes* teach relativism, the dependence of all opinions

and values on local or historical circumstance, especially
nationality, does not seem entirely correct. If it were, Rica and
Usbek would surely be unable to adjust to France. The fact that they
do adjust indicates that, in Montesquieu's eyes, there are some
values which transcend particular circumstances.

Neither Rica nor Usbek provides a convenient summing-up of
what they have learned, but the distance they travel can be
measured, in some degree, by looking at a few of the obvious
contrasts between the virtues of Europe and the defects of Asia:
brutality and caprice are associated with the Persian government,
mildness and justice (usually) with the French; ignorance and
superstition with Persia, knowledge and reason with France,
although Usbek is a rationalist before he arrives in France, and finds
much there that is irrational; suspicion and secrecy with the social
life of the East, openness and gregariousness with France,
sometimes to excess; economic backwardness and apathy with the
East, prosperity and industriousness with Europe. It would be too
simple to say, however, that the Persians leave the bad behind in
Asia and find the good in France. Being loyal Muslims, it seems to
them that European Christianity is full of conflict and disaffection.
On women and marriage, Persia takes the male demand for
women's chastity to excess, inspiring revolt; however, French
permissiveness does not appeal to Usbek, whatever Rica may think.
In politics, the monarchical system in France is a middle term, lying
between the despotism of Asia and the freedom of the republics.

It is especially difficult to fit utilitarian values into a straightforward pattern of contrast between East and West. In the widest
sense, that of the good of an entire society, utility is disregarded in
Asia, but it is not constantly respected in France; Law's 'Système'
has been allowed, as it seems, to demoralise society beyond
redemption. Before the diatribe in Letter CXLVI, much in France
has been praised for its social value, but much too has been
criticised. Whether the Persians react with approval or not, their
standpoint is that of citizens whose interest lies with the welfare of
the social group of which they are temporary or permanent
members, whether it is the human race as a whole, in the letters on

depopulation, or visitors to a *salon* who are bored by some conceited fool.

It is not at all clear whether, having come in order to study Western knowledge, the Persians can be said to complete their studies. Usbek announces unhappily that he must leave France in Letter CLV, dated October 1719; but in November 1720 he is still there to write Letter CXLVI. Was this an oversight on Montesquieu's part, or should we deduce that Usbek changed his mind? A textual variant suggest that he stays in France. In the second edition, Letter CXLVI was dated July 1720, not November as in the first. Montesquieu must therefore have considered the dates at a very late stage. Whichever edition has primacy, Usbek's statement in Letter CLV that he will leave seems not to have been followed up.

Rica does not want to leave at all, and in view of his greater ease in adapting himself to French life it is a reasonable supposition that he prefers to remain, whatever Usbek's decision. Not wholly frivolously, I mention another consideration: a mystery surrounds the many letters addressed by Rica to '***' (there are only three such from Usbek), and it is a plausible hypothesis that they are supposed to have been sent to a lady whose identity is tactfully concealed; most of the subjects seem appropriate. It may be that Rica keeps Usbek in France because he has a romantic liaison, having taken advantage of the freedom allowed to French women and the lack of jealousy of their husbands, described so vividly in Letter LV.

However that may be, much indeterminacy surrounds the conclusion of the Persians' stay. On the subject of intellectual life, the final remarks come from Usbek, again downcast, in Letter CXLV. The *homme d'esprit*, he says, is unpopular, while learned men and scientists risk persecution on religious or political grounds, as well as for more trivial reasons. He goes on to contrast government propagandists, manipulating facts for personal advancement, with historians who have 'de la noblesse dans l'esprit et quelque droiture dans le cœur'. In the light of the letters on history and political freedom, not to mention the controversy aroused much later

by the *Esprit des lois*, it is almost as if Montesquieu were anticipat-
ing the difficulties that he was to face in his later career. At the time
of Letter CXLV, however, the reference was more likely to have
been to a historian friend, not to his own prospects; Nicolas Fréret
had been imprisoned in 1716 for criticising a Jesuit's work on
history (*25*, p.11). The tone of Letter CXLV adds to the atmosphere
of pessimism that characterises the last observations on France, in
Letter CXLVI, and Usbek's future in Persia, forecast in Letter CLV.
It is an oddly unhappy ending for a work that contains so much
liveliness and humour. If the despondency was due to personal
circumstances, or disillusionment at the results of Law's 'Système',
let us hope that the public's warm reception of the *Lettres persanes*
dispelled the mood.

Bibliography

The following is a selective list of editions, books and articles that I have used or recommend for further reading. The italicised numbers are those by which the items are referred to above. A full bibliography of the *Lettres persanes* is to be found in: Louis Desgraves, *Répertoire des ouvrages et articles sur Montesquieu*, Geneva, Droz, 1988, pp.166–85. The critical editions both give the 1758 text, which included Montesquieu's late revisions. Adam's is preferable for textual correctness, Vernière's for the fullness of the introduction and annotation.

EDITIONS

1. Montesquieu, *Lettres persanes*, critical edition by Antoine Adam, Textes littéraires français (Geneva, Droz, 1954).
2. ——, *Lettres persanes*, critical edition by Paul Vernière, Classiques Garnier (Paris, 1960).

STUDIES

3. Barrière, P., 'Les éléments personnels et les éléments bordelais dans les *Lettres persanes*', *Revue d'histoire littéraire de la France*, LI (1951), 17–36.
4. Betts, C.J., *Early Deism in France* (The Hague, Nijhoff, 1984).
5. Braudel, F., and Labrousse, E., eds, *Histoire économique et sociale de la France*, Vol. II, *Des derniers temps de l'âge seigneurial aux préludes de l'âge industriel (1660–1789)*, by Ernest Labrousse and others (Paris, P.U.F., 1970).
6. Crisafulli, Alessandro, 'Montesquieu's Story of the Troglodytes, Its Background, Meaning and Significance', *Publications of the Modern Language Association of America*, LVIII (1943), 372–92.
7. Dedieu, Joseph, *Montesquieu, l'homme et l'œuvre* (Paris, Boivin, 1943).
8. Desgraves, Louis, *Montesquieu* (Paris, Mazarine, 1986).
9. Dufrénoy, Marie-Louise, *L'Orient romanesque en France, 1704–1789*, 2 vols, Vol. I (Montreal, Fides, 1946).
10. *Europe*, 574 (1977), issue devoted to Montesquieu (includes:

G. Benrekassa, 'Le parcours idéologique des *Lettres persanes*', 60–79; C. Dauphiné, 'Pourquoi un roman du sérail?', 89–96; M. Delon, 'Un monde d'eunuques', 79–88).

11. Ford, F.L., *Robe and Sword: The Regrouping of the French Aristocracy after Louis XIV* (Cambridge, Massachusetts, Harvard U.P., 1953).

12. Funck-Brentano, Frantz, *La Régence* (Paris, Tallandier, 1931).

13. Geffriaud-Rosso, Jeanne, *Montesquieu et la féminité* (Pisa, Goliardica, 1977).

14. Goubert, Pierre, *L'Ancien Régime*, Vol. I, *La société* (Paris, Colin, 1969).

15. Grosrichard, Alain, *Structure du sérail: la fiction du despotisme asiatique dans l'Occident classique* (Paris, Seuil, 1979).

16. Gunny, Ahmad, 'Montesquieu's View of Islam in the *Lettres persanes*', *Studies on Voltaire and the Eighteenth Century*, CLXXIV (Oxford, Voltaire Foundation, 1978).

17. Lavisse, Ernest, ed., *Histoire de France illustrée, depuis les origines jusqu'à la Révolution*, Vol. VIII, 2, *Louis XV (1715–1774)*, by Henri Carré (Paris, Hachette, 1911).

18. Mandrou, R., *La France aux XVIIe et XVIIIe siècles* (Paris, P.U.F., 1970).

19. Mason, Haydn, *French Writers and their Society 1715–1800* (London, Macmillan, 1982).

20. Mass, Edgar, *Literatur und Zensur in der frühen Aufklärung: Produktion, Distribution und Rezeption der 'Lettres persanes'*, Analecta Romanica, 46 (Frankfurt, Klostermann, 1981).

21. Meyer, Jean, *La Vie quotidienne en France au temps de la Régence* (Paris, Hachette, 1979).

22. Mousnier, Roland, *Les Institutions de la France sous la monarchie absolue, 1598–1789*, 2 vols, Vol. I, *Société et état* (Paris, P.U.F., 1974).

23. Roddick, Nick, 'The Structure of the *Lettres persanes*', *French Studies*, XXVIII (1974), 396–407.

24. van Roosbroeck, G.L., *Persian Letters before Montesquieu*, New York, Columbia U.P., 1932.

25. Shackleton, Robert, *Montesquieu, A Critical Biography* (Oxford, U.P., 1961).

26. ——, 'The Moslem Chronology of the *Lettres persanes*', *French Studies*, VIII (1954), 17–27.

27. Starobinski, Jean, *Montesquieu par lui-même* (Paris, Seuil, 1953).

28. Todorov, Tzvetan, 'Réflexions sur les *Lettres persanes*', *Romanic Review*, LXXIV (1983), 306–15.

29. Vantuch, Anton, 'Les éléments personnels dans les *Lettres persanes*',

Annales de la faculté des lettres et sciences humaines de Nice, VIII (1969), 127–42.

30. Vartanian, Aram, 'Eroticism and Politics in the *Lettres persanes*', *Romanic Review*, LX (1969), 23–33.
31. Véquaud, Alain, *Les 'Lettres persanes', Montesquieu: Analyse critique* (Paris, Hatier, 1983).
32. Waddicor, Mark, *Montesquieu: Lettres persanes*, Studies in French Literature, 31 (London, Arnold, 1977).
33. Young, D.B., 'Libertarian Demography: Montesquieu's Essay on Depopulation in the *Lettres persanes*', *Journal of the History of Ideas*, XXXVI (1975), 669–82.

ADDENDA

34. Hoffman, P., 'Usbek métaphysicien. Recherches sur la signification de la 69e "Lettre persane"', *Revue d'histoire littéraire de la France*, XCII (1992), 779–800.
35. Mallinson, G.J., 'Usbek, Language and Power: Images of Authority in Montesquieu's *Lettres persanes*', *French Forum*, XVIII (1993), 23–36.

CRITICAL GUIDES TO FRENCH TEXTS

edited by

Roger Little, Wolfgang van Emden, David Williams

QUEEN MARY & WESTFIELD
COLLEGE LIBRARY
(MILE END)

PQ 2086 . L5 FILE

PQ 2011.L6 BET

QMW Library

23 1085157 7

MAIN LIBRARY
QUEEN MARY, UNIVERSITY OF LONDON
Mile End Road, London E1 4NS
DATE DUE FOR RETURN

1 0 FEB 2003

2 4 FEB 2005

- 3 OCT 2003

WITHDRAWN
FROM STOCK
QMUL LIBRARY

2 7 NOV 2003

3 1 MAR 2004

3 0 APR 2004

3 1 MAY 2005